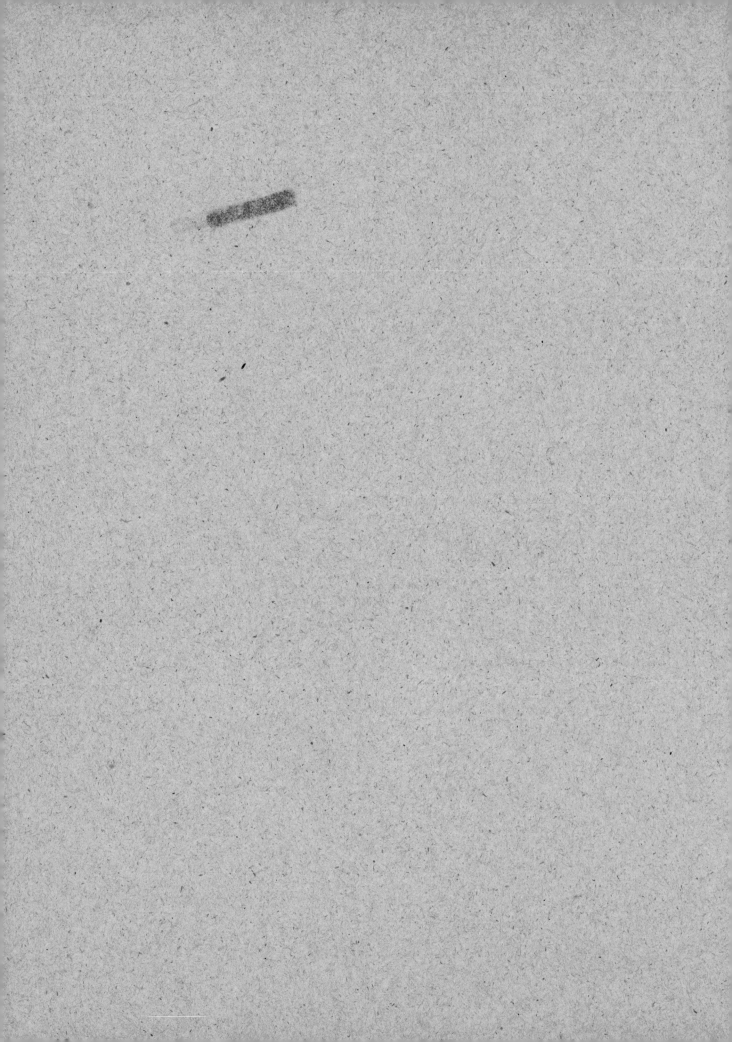

THE PRESIDENTS

Editor

Fred L. Israel

VOLUME 4

Rutherford B. Hayes 1877 – William McKinley 1901

Grolier Educational

SHERMAN TURNPIKE, DANBURY, CONNECTICUT

The publisher gratefully acknowledges permission from the sources to reproduce photos that appear on the cover.

Volume 1
J. Adams – New York Historical Society
J. Monroe – Library of Congress

Volume 2
J. K. Polk; A. Jackson; J. Tyler – Library of Congress
J. Q. Adams – National Archives

Volume 3
U. S. Grant – National Archives
A. Johnson; Z. Taylor – Library of Congress

Volume 4
B. Harrison; W. McKinley; J. A. Garfield – Library of Congress

Volume 5
H. Hoover; W. G. Harding – Library of Congress
T. Roosevelt – National Archives

Volume 6
D. D. Eisenhower – Library of Congress
L. B. Johnson – White House

Volume 7
B. Clinton – The White House
R. Reagan – Bush/Reagan Committee
G. Bush – Cynthia Johnson, The White House

Volume 8
T. Roosevelt – National Archives
B. Clinton – The White House

Published 1997 exclusively for the school and library market by Grolier Educational

Sherman Turnpike, Danbury, Connecticut

© 1997 by Charles E. Smith Books, Inc.

Set: ISBN 0-7172-7642-2

Volume 4: ISBN 0-7172-7646-5

Library of Congress number:

The presidents.

   p. cm.

   Contents: v. 1. 1789–1825 (Washington–Monroe) — v. 2. 1825–1849 (Adams–Polk)

   v. 3. 1849–1877 (Taylor–Grant) — v. 4. 1877–1901 (Hayes–McKinley) — v. 5.1901–1933 (T. Roosevelt–Hoover)

   v. 6. 1933–1969 (F. D. Roosevelt–L. B. Johnson) — v. 7. 1969–1997 (Nixon–Clinton)

   v. 8. Documents, suggested reading, charts, tables, appendixes

1. Presidents – United States – Juvenile literature.

[1. Presidents.]   96-31491

E176.1.P9175   1997   CIP

973.099 — dc20   AC

For information, address the publisher

Grolier Educational, Sherman Turnpike, Danbury, Connecticut 06816

Printed in the United States of America

Cover design by Smart Graphics

TABLE OF CONTENTS

VOLUME FOUR

CONTRIBUTORS

EDITOR

Fred L. Israel received his Ph.D. from Columbia University. He has written several books for young adults including *Franklin D. Roosevelt, Henry Kissinger,* and *Know Your Government: The FBI.* Dr. Israel is also the editor of *History of American Presidential Elections, 1789–1968, The Chief Executive: Inaugural Addresses of the Presidents from George Washington to Lyndon Johnson,* and *The State of the Union Messages of the Presidents of the United States.* His most recent book is *Running for President, The Candidates and Their Images,* a two-volume work with Arthur M. Schlesinger, Jr. and David J. Frent.

Dr. Israel is Professor, Department of History, The City College of the City University of New York.

CONTRIBUTORS

Donald C. Bacon is a Washington-based journalist specializing in the presidency and Congress. He served as staff writer of *The Wall Street Journal* and assistant managing editor of *U.S. News and World Report.* A former Congressional Fellow, he is the author of *Rayburn: A Biography* and *Congress and You.* He is coeditor of *The Encyclopedia of the United States Congress.*

Hendrik Booraem V received his Ph.D. from The Johns Hopkins University. He taught social studies at Strom Thurmond High School, South Carolina, for many years. He has been Adjunct Professor at Rutgers University, Camden, Alvernia College, Lehigh University, and the State University of New York at Purchase. Dr. Booraem is the author of *The Formation of the Republican Party in New York: Politics and Conscience in the Antebellum North, The Road to Respectability: James A. Garfield and His World, 1844–1852,* and *The Provincial: Calvin Coolidge and His World, 1885–1895.*

Thomas Bracken received his B.A. and M.A., summa cum laude, from The City College of the City University of New York. He is currently enrolled in the doctoral program there, and he is Adjunct Professor of History.

David Burner received his Ph.D. from Columbia University. He is Professor of American History at the State University of New York at Stony Brook. Among Dr. Burner's many publications are *John F. Kennedy and a New Generation, The Torch is Passed: The Kennedy Brothers and American Liberalism* (with Thomas R. West) and *The Politics of Provincialism: The Democratic Party in Transition, 1918–1932.* He is also the coauthor of *Firsthand America: A History of the United States.*

Gary Cohn received his M.A. in Popular Culture Studies from Bowling Green State University in 1980 and has completed course work towards the doctorate in American History at the State University of New York at Stony Brook. As an Adjunct Professor he has taught history at The City College of the City University of New York and creative writing and composition at the C.W. Post campus of Long Island University.

Richard Nelson Current is University Distinguished Professor of History, Emeritus, at the University of North Carolina, Greensboro and former President of the Southern Historical Association. Among Dr. Current's many books are *Speaking of Abraham Lincoln: The Man and His Meaning for Our Times, Lincoln and the First Shot, The Lincoln Nobody Knows, Lincoln the President: Last Full Measure,* and with T. Harry Williams and Frank Freidel, *American History: A Survey.*

James B. Gardner received his Ph.D. from Vanderbilt University. He has been Deputy Executive Director of the American Historical Association since 1986 and Acting Executive Director of that organization since 1994. Dr. Gardner was with the American Association for State and Local History from 1979 to 1986, where he served in a variety of capacities, including Director of Education and Special Programs. Among his many publications is *A Historical Guide to the United States.*

Anne-Marie Grimaud received her B.A. from the Sorbonne, Paris and her M.A. from the State University of New York at Stony Brook, where she is currently enrolled in the doctoral program in American History.

Douglas Kinnard graduated from the United States Military Academy and served in Europe during World War II. He also served in Korea and Vietnam and retired as Brigadier General. He then received his Ph.D. from Princeton University. Dr. Kinnard is Professor Emeritus, University of Vermont and was Chief of Military History, U.S. Army. Among Dr. Kinnard's books are *Ike 1890–1990: A Pictorial History, President Eisenhower and Strategy Management: A Study in Defense Politics,* and *Maxwell Taylor and The American Experience in Vietnam.*

Robert A. Raber received his J.D. from the Law School, University of California, Berkeley. He retired from law practice and received his M.A. from The City College of the City University of New York, where he is enrolled in the doctoral program.

Donald A. Ritchie received his Ph.D. from the University of Maryland. Dr. Ritchie is on the Executive Committee of the American Historical Association, and he has been Associate Historian, United States Senate for 20 years. Among his many publications are *Press Gallery: Congress and the Washington Correspondents, The Young Oxford Companion to the Congress of the United States,* and *Oxford Profiles of American Journalists.*

Robert A. Rutland is Professor of History Emeritus, University of Virginia. He was editor in chief of *The Papers of James Madison* for many years, and he was coordinator of bicentennial programs at the Library of Congress from 1969 to 1971. Dr. Rutland is the author of many books including *Madison's Alternatives: The Jeffersonian Republicans and the Coming of War, 1805–1812, James Madison and the Search for Nationhood, James Madison: The Founding Father,* and *The Presidency of James Madison.* He is editor of *James Madison and the American Nation, 1751–1836: An Encyclopedia.*

Raymond W. Smock received his Ph.D. from the University of Maryland. He was involved with the Booker T. Washington Papers Project for many years and was coeditor from 1975 to 1983. He was Historian, Office of the Bicentennial, U.S. House of Representatives. In 1983, he was appointed as the first Director of the Office of the Historian of the U.S. House of Representatives. Among the major publications of that office are *The Biographical Directory of the United States Congress, 1774–1989, Black Americans in Congress, 1877–1989,* and *Women in Congress, 1917–1990.*

Darren D. Staloff received his Ph.D. from Columbia University, and he was a Post-Doctoral Fellow at the Institute of Early American History and Culture. He has taught at the College of Staten Island, Columbia University, and the College of William and Mary. Dr. Staloff is currently Assistant Professor of American History, The City College of the City University of New York. He is the author of *The Making of an American Thinking Class: Intellectuals and Intelligentsia in Puritan Massachusetts.*

John Stern received his M.A. from the State University of New York at Stony Brook, where he is enrolled in the doctoral program. His thesis is on Eugene McCarthy and the Presidential Campaign of 1968.

Edmund B. Sullivan received his Ed.D. from Fitchburg State College. He was Principal, New Hampton Community School, New Hampshire, and he taught at the North Adams and Newton public schools in Massachusetts. Dr. Sullivan was Professor at American International College and University of Hartford, and he was the founding Director and Curator of the Museum of American Political Life, West Hartford Connecticut. He is the author of *American Political Ribbons and Ribbon Badges, 1828–1988, American Political Badges and Medalets, 1789–1892,* and *Collecting Political Americana.*

Linda S. Vertrees received her B.A. in History from Western Illinois University and her M.A. in Library Science from the University of Chicago. She has written several annotated lists of suggested readings including the one for *The Holocaust, A Grolier Student Library.*

Thomas R. West received his Ph.D. from the Columbia University. He is Associate Professor, Department of History, Catholic University. He is coauthor, with David Burner, of *The Torch is Passed: The Kennedy Brothers and American Liberalism* and *Column Right: Conservative Journalists in the Service of Nationalism.*

INTRODUCTION

No branch of the federal government caused the authors of the Constitution as many problems as did the Executive. They feared a strong chief of state. After all, the American Revolution was, in part, a struggle against the King of England and the powerful royal governors. Surprisingly though, much power was granted to the president of the United States who is responsible only to the people. This was the boldest feature of the new Constitution. The president has varied duties. Above all, he must take care that the laws be faithfully executed. And also according to the Constitution, the president:

- is the commander in chief of the armed forces;
- has the power to make treaties with other nations (with the Senate's consent);
- appoints Supreme Court Justices and other members of the federal courts, ambassadors to other countries, department heads, and other high officials (all with the Senate's consent);
- signs into law or vetoes bills passed by Congress;
- calls special sessions of Congress in times of emergency.

In some countries, the power to lead is inherited. In others, men seize power through force. But in the United States, the people choose the nation's leader. The power of all the people to elect the president was not stated in the original Constitution. This came later. The United States is the first nation to have an elected president—and a president with a stated term of office. Every four years since the adoption of the Constitution in 1789, the nation has held a presidential election. Elections have been held even during major economic disruptions and wars. Indeed, these elections every four years are a vivid reminder of our democratic roots.

Who can vote for president of the United States? The original Constitution left voting qualifications to the states. At first, the states limited voting to white and very few black men who owned a certain amount of property. It was argued that only those with an economic or commercial interest in the nation should have a say in who could run the government. After the Civil War (1861–1865), the Fourteenth (1868) and Fifteenth (1870) Amendments to the Constitution guaranteed the vote to all men over the age of 21. The guarantee was only in theory. The Nineteenth Amendment (1920) extended the right to vote to women. The Nineteenth Amendment was a victory of the woman's suffrage movement which had worked for many years to achieve this goal. In 1964, the Twenty-fourth Amendment abolished poll taxes—a fee paid before a citizen was allowed to vote. This tax had kept many poor people, both black and white, from voting in several Southern states. And, the Twenty-sixth Amendment (1971) lowered the voting age to 18. (See Volume 8 for the complete text of the Constitution.)

In 1965, Congress passed the Voting Rights Act; it was renewed in 1985. This law, which carried out the requirements of the Fifteenth Amendment, made it illegal to interfere with anyone's right to vote. It forbade the use of literacy tests and, most important, the law mandated that federal voter registrars be sent into counties where less than 50 percent of the voting age population (black and white) was registered. This assumed that there must be serious barriers based on prejudice if so few had registered to vote. Those who had prevented African Americans from voting through fear and threat of violence now had to face the force of the federal government. Immediately, the number of African American voters in Southern states jumped dramatically from about 35 percent to 65 percent. In 1970, 1975, and 1982, Congress added amendments to the Voting Rights Act which helped other minorities such as Hispanics, Asians, Native Americans, and

Eskimos. For example, states must provide bilingual ballots in counties in which 5 percent or more of the population does not speak or read English. Today any citizen over the age of 18 has the right to vote in a presidential election. Many would argue that this is not only a right but also an obligation. However, all states deny the right to vote to anyone who is in prison.

Who can be president of the United States? There are formal constitutional requirements: one must be a "natural born citizen," at least 35 years old, and a resident of the United States for 14 years. The Constitution refers to the president as "he." It was probably beyond the thought process of the Founding Fathers that a woman, or a man who was not white, would ever be considered. The Twenty-second Amendment (1951), which deals with term limitations, uses "person" in referring to the president, recognizing that a woman could serve in that office.

How is the president elected? Most Americans assume that the president is elected by popular vote and the candidate with the highest number wins the election. This is not correct and may surprise those who thought they voted for Bill Clinton, Robert Dole, or Ross Perot in 1996. In fact, they voted for Clinton's or Dole's or Perot's electors who then elected the president. In the United States, the voters do not directly select the president. The Constitution provides a fairly complex—and some argue, an outdated—procedure for electing the president. Indeed, the electoral system devised by the Framers and modified by the Twelfth Amendment (1804) is unique. The records of the Constitutional Convention (1787) are silent in explaining the origins of the electoral system, usually referred to as the Electoral College. The several Federalist papers (Nos. 68–71) written by Alexander Hamilton in defense of the electoral system omit any source for the idea.

Under the electoral system of the United States, each state has the number of electoral voters equal to the size of its congressional delegation (House of Representatives plus Senate). Every 10 years, the census, as required by the Constitution, adjusts the number of representatives each state has in the House of Representatives because of population growth or loss. Every state always must have two senators. In the presidential election of 1996, for example, New York State had 33 electoral votes, because New York has 31 representatives and two senators. Alaska had three electoral votes, because Alaska has one representative and two senators. Since every congressional district must be approximately equal in population, we can say that the entire population of Alaska—the largest state in geographic size—is approximately equal in population to the 19th congressional district of New York City which covers the upper part of Manhattan Island.

There are 435 members of the House of Representatives. This number was fixed in 1910. There are 100 members of the Senate (50 states x 2 senators). This equals 535 electors. The Twenty-third Amendment (1961) gives the District of Columbia, the seat of our nation's capital, the electoral vote of the least populous state, three. So, the total electoral vote is 535 plus three or 538. To be elected president, a candidate must receive a majority, that is more than 50 percent, of the electoral votes: 270 electoral votes. If no candidate obtains a majority, the House of Representatives must choose the president from the top three candidates with each state delegation casting one vote. This happened in the 1824 presidential election. (See the article on John Quincy Adams.)

How does a political party choose its presidential nominee? Political parties play a crucial role—they select the candidates and provide the voters with a choice of alternatives.

In the early days of the Republic, the party's membership in Congress—the congressional caucus—chose presidential nominees. Sometimes state and local officials also put forward candidates. National party conventions where delegates were selected by state and local groups began by the 1830s. Each state had different delegate election procedures—some more democratic than others. Custom dictated that the convention sought the candidate. Potential nominees invariably seemed withdrawn and disinterested. They would rarely attend a nominating convention. Any attempt to pursue delegates was considered to be in bad taste. In fact, custom dictated that an official delegation went to the nominee's home to notify him of the party's decision and ask if he would accept. In the early years, convention officials sent a letter. By 1852, the candidate was informed in person. In the 1890s, these notification ceremonies dramatically increased in size. Madison Square Garden in New York City was the site for Grover Cleveland's 1892 notification.

By the first decade of the twentieth century, political reformers considered the convention system most undemocratic. They felt that it was a system dominated by patronage seeking party bosses who ignored the average voter. The primary system began as a way to increase participation in the nominating process. Candidates for the nation's highest office now actually sought the support of convention delegates. Theoretically, the primary allows all party members to choose their party's nominee. Most twentieth century conventions though, have seen a combination of delegates chosen by a political machine and elected in a primary. Today success in the primaries virtually assures the nomination. With few exceptions, the national conventions have become a rubber stamp for the candidate who did the best in the primaries.

The Campaign and Election. The presidential campaign is the great democratic exercise in politics. In recent elections, televised debates between the candidates have become a ritual, attracting record numbers of viewers. Public opinion polls continually monitor the nation's pulse. Commentators and writers analyze campaign strategies. Perhaps the winning strategy is to mobilize the party faithful and to persuade the independent voter that their candidate is the best. This is a costly process and since 1976, the general treasury provides major financial assistance to presidential campaigns. Public funding helps serious presidential candidates to present their qualifications without selling out to wealthy contributors and special interest groups.

Finally, on that first Tuesday after the first Monday in November, the voters make their choice. With the tragic exception of 1860, the American people have accepted the results. (See the article on Abraham Lincoln.) The election process works. Democracy has survived. Forty-one men have held the office of president of the United States. Each has been a powerful personality with varied leadership traits. Each had the opportunity to make major decisions both in foreign and domestic matters which affected the direction of the nation.

Join us as we proceed to study the men who helped to shape our history. We will also learn about their vice presidents, their cabinets, their families, and their homes and monuments.

Fred L. Israel
The City College of the City University of New York

Acknowledgments

Sir Isaac Newton, the seventeenth-century English scientist who created calculus, discovered that white light is composed of many colors, discovered the law of gravity, and developed the standard laws of motion, once said, "If I have seen farther, it is because I have stood on the shoulders of giants." He meant that he used the work of those who came before him as a starting point for the development of his own ideas. This concept is as true in reference books as it is in science.

The White House Historical Association (740 Jackson Place N.W., Washington, D.C. 20503) supplied all the full page color paintings of the presidents, except seven. They are used with the permission of the White House

Historical Association, and we are grateful to them for their cooperation. The painting of James Monroe is Courtesy of the James Monroe Museum and Memorial Library, Fredericksburg, Virginia; the William Henry Harrison portrait is Courtesy of Grouseland; the John Tyler painting is Courtesy of Sherwood Forest Plantation; the Benjamin Harrison painting is from the President Benjamin Harrison Home; Harry Truman's photograph is from the U.S. Navy, Courtesy Harry S. Truman Library; George Bush's photograph is Courtesy of the Bush Presidential Materials Project; Bill Clinton's photograph is Courtesy of The White House. All the busts of the vice presidents are Courtesy of the Architect of the Capitol.

Over three dozen illustrations are credited to the Collection of David J. and Janice L. Frent. The Frents are friends and neighbors. Fred Israel and I both want to thank them very much for allowing us to show some of the treasures of their unequaled collection of political memorabilia.

The authors of the biographical pieces on the presidents are listed in each volume. They have provided the core of this work, and I am very grateful to them for their cooperation. Dr. Donald A. Ritchie, Associate Historian, United States Senate, wrote all the biographies of the vice presidents. Few people know more about this subject than Dr. Ritchie, and we appreciate his assistance.

Maribeth A. Corona (Editor, Charles E. Smith Books, Inc.) and I have written the sections on Family, Cabinet, and Places. Dr. Israel's editing of our work corrected and improved it greatly although we take full responsibility for any errors that remain. In preparing the material on places, three books served as a starting point: *Presidential Libraries and Museums, An Illustrated Guide,* Pat Hyland (Congressional Quarterly Inc., 1995); *Historic Homes of the American Presidents,* second edition, Irvin Haas (Dover Publications, 1991); and *Cabins, Cottages & Mansions, Homes of the Presidents of the United States,* Nancy D. Myers Benbow and Christopher H. Benbow (Thomas Publications, 1993). We wrote to every place noted in this work and our copy is based on the wealth of information returned to us. It is the most comprehensive and up-to-date collection of information available on this subject.

There is no single book on the families of the presidents. We relied on the abundance of biographies and autobiographies of members of the first families. Also helpful was *Children in the White House,* Christine Sadler (G.P. Putnam's Sons, 1967); *The Presidents' Mothers,* Doris Faber (St. Martin's Press, 1978); and *The First Ladies,* Margaret Brown Klapthor (White House Historical Association, 1989).

The Complete Book of U.S. Presidents, William A. DeGregorio (Wings Books, 1993) is an outstanding one-volume reference work, and we referred to it often. I also had the great pleasure of referring often to three encyclopedias which I had published earlier: *Encyclopedia of the American Presidency,* Leonard W. Levy and Louis Fisher (Simon & Schuster, 1994); *Encyclopedia of the American Constitution,* Leonard W. Levy, Kenneth L. Karst, and Dennis Mahoney (Macmillan & Free Press, 1986); and *Encyclopedia of the United States Congress,* Donald C. Bacon, Roger Davidson, and Morton H. Keller (Simon & Schuster, 1995). I also referred often to *Running for President, The Candidates and Their Images,* Arthur M. Schlesinger, Jr. (Simon & Schuster, 1994). Publishing this two-volume set also gave me the pleasure of working with Professor Schlesinger and the Associate Editors, Fred L. Israel and David J. Frent.

Most of the copyediting was done by Jerilyn Famighetti who was, as usual, prompt, accurate, and pleasant. Our partner in this endeavor was M.E. Aslett Corporation, 95 Campus Plaza, Edison, New Jersey. Although everyone at Aslett lent a hand, special thanks go to Elizabeth Geary, who designed the books; Brian Hewitt and Bob Bovasso, who scanned the images; and Joanne Morbit, who composed the pages. They designed every page and prepared the film for printing. The index was prepared by Jacqueline Flamm.

Charles E. Smith
Freehold, New Jersey

Rutherford B. Hayes

19TH PRESIDENT

OF THE UNITED STATES OF AMERICA

CHRONOLOGICAL EVENTS

4 October 1822	Born, Delaware, Ohio
3 August 1842	Graduated from Kenyon College, Gambier, Ohio
27 August 1845	Graduated from Harvard Law School, Cambridge, Massachusetts
March 1845	Admitted to bar, Ohio
1858	Appointed city solicitor by Cincinnati city council
1859	Elected city solicitor
27 June 1861	Commissioned as major in Twenty-third Ohio Volunteer Infantry
24 October 1861	Promoted to lieutenant colonel
24 October 1862	Promoted to colonel
October 1864	Elected to U.S. House of Representatives
13 March 1865	Promoted to brevet major general
8 June 1865	Resigned from Union army
4 December 1865	Began term in U.S. House of Representatives
1866	Reelected to U.S. House of Representatives
1867 and 1869	Elected governor of Ohio
1875	Again elected governor of Ohio
2 March 1877	Declared president by Electoral Commission
5 March 1877	Inaugurated president
March–April 1877	Withdrawal of federal troops from the South
28 February 1878	Vetoed Bland-Allison Silver Purchase Bill
17 November 1880	Chinese Exclusion Act signed
March 1881	Retired to Fremont, Ohio
1883	Named president of National Prison Association
17 January 1893	Died, Fremont, Ohio

BIOGRAPHY

The circumstances that led to Rutherford B. Hayes's election were the most unusual for any president in U.S. history. The electoral votes of three Southern states and one vote from Oregon were disputed. Hayes needed all the disputed votes to win the election—and he received them.

Hayes was born on 4 October 1822, in Delaware, Ohio. His father, Rutherford Hayes, died a few months before he was born, and his mother, Sophia Birchard Hayes, and her youngest brother, Sardis Birchard, raised Hayes and his older sister, Fanny.

EARLY CAREER. Hayes attended schools in Norwalk, Ohio and in Middletown, Connecticut.

Once the Civil War began, Hayes made speeches, recruited men, and accepted the rank of major in the Twenty-third Ohio Volunteer Infantry. He said, "I would prefer to go into it if I knew that I was to die or be killed in the course of it than to live through and after it without taking any part in it." Hayes served four years, was wounded four times, and was breveted (temporarily promoted) to major general in 1865. (Courtesy Library of Congress.)

In 1842, he graduated from Kenyon College first in his class. After studying law for a year in Columbus, Ohio, he entered Harvard Law School in 1843, graduating in 1845. He returned to Ohio and began a successful law practice. In 1852, Hayes married Lucy Ware Webb, a graduate of Wesleyan Women's College in Cincinnati. Later, she became the first First Lady to have a college degree. She was a devout Methodist and a strong opponent of slavery. Because of her influence, Hayes defended runaway slaves. He joined the Republican Party when it was formed in the mid-1850's and supported Abraham Lincoln in the 1860 presidential election. His first public office was city solicitor for Cincinnati (1858–1861). In June 1861, Hayes enlisted in the Twenty-third Ohio Volunteer Infantry and was commissioned as a major. He was promoted to lieutenant colonel in October 1861 and to colonel in October 1862 after he led a decisive charge at the Battle of South Mountain, Maryland, despite a serious arm wound. In October 1864, after the Battle of Cedar Creek, Virginia, where he was wounded for the fourth time, he was promoted to brigadier general.

In August 1864, while still in the army, he was nominated for the U.S. House of Representatives. Hayes accepted the nomination but refused to campaign. When Ohio Republican leaders suggested that he take a leave from the army, Hayes replied, "An officer fit for duty, who at this crisis would abandon his post to electioneer for a seat in Congress, ought to be scalped." This statement and his devotion to duty impressed voters, and he easily won the election. Hayes still refused to leave the army until the war was over. On 8 June 1865, Hayes, now a major general, finally resigned his commission. In Congress from 1865 to 1867, Hayes chaired the Joint Committee on the Library. During his tenure, the holdings of the Library of Congress were expanded, and he worked hard to make the Library into a great institution. Hayes supported the Radical Republicans and their plan to punish the former rebel states and to establish political institutions that would

respect the rights of former slaves. He voted for the impeachment of Andrew Johnson in 1868.

Twice elected governor of Ohio, he served from 1868 to 1872. His greatest achievements, he thought, were Ohio's ratification of the Fifteenth Amendment, which extended the right to vote to African American males, and the establishment of

AMENDMENT XV

SECTION 1. The right of citizens of the United States to vote shall not be denied or abridged by the United States or by any State on account of race, color, or previous condition of servitude.

SECTION 2. The Congress shall have power to enforce this article by appropriate legislation.

• *For the complete text of the Constitution, see Volume 8.*

The Ohio State University. Hayes had been a popular governor and Republicans urged him to run a third time, but he honored Ohio's practice of having governors serve no more than two consecutive terms. He retired to his estate near Fremont, Ohio, which he had inherited from an uncle. In 1875, Ohio Republican leaders, worried about the prospect of substantial Democratic congressional gains because of the corruption of the national Republican administration, drafted Hayes for governor once again. His narrow victory over the incumbent Democratic governor gave him national visibility as a potential Republican presidential candidate.

HAYES-TILDEN ELECTION OF 1876. The Republican National Convention opened in Cincinnati, Ohio on 14 June 1876. Representative James G. Blaine of Maine led on the early balloting but fell short of the number of votes required for nomination. Blaine's opponents recognized

President and Mrs. Hayes celebrated their 25th wedding anniversary with a reception in the White House. She was the first First Lady to have earned a college degree. She started the custom of the Easter egg roll on the White House Lawn. (Courtesy Collection of David J. and Janice L. Frent.)

that they had to unite behind a single candidate. They chose Hayes because he was not controversial and he was free of scandal. Hayes received the nomination on the seventh ballot.

The campaign between Hayes and the Democratic candidate, New York Governor Samuel J. Tilden, focused on their different views of polit-

This is a salesman's sample of campaign ribbons used to get orders. The Democrats, Samuel J. Tilden and Thomas A. Hendricks (left), received 51 percent of the popular vote. However, the Republicans, Rutherford B. Hayes and William A. Wheeler, received one more vote in the Electoral College. (Courtesy Collection of David J. and Janice L. Frent.)

ical reform. Tilden attacked the Republicans for the corruption of the Grant administration. (By early 1876, several members of Grant's cabinet had resigned facing charges of bribery and corruption.) Hayes countered with the familiar Republican campaign technique of "waving the bloody shirt" (see below) suggesting that Southern Democrats had committed treason in seceding from the Union and causing the Civil War.

The November election produced one of the most controversial results in U.S. history. Tilden received a majority of the popular votes, but he was one vote short of the needed majority in the Electoral College to be declared the winner. In three Southern states—South Carolina, Florida, and Louisiana—Republican leaders challenged

"Bloody shirt" rhetoric hit a new low when Robert Ingersoll spoke to a convention of Union veterans of the Civil War: "Every man that tried to destroy this nation was a Democrat. Every man that loved slavery better than liberty was a Democrat. The man that assassinated Abraham Lincoln was a Democrat . . . Soldiers, every scar you have on your heroic bodies was given to you by a Democrat."

• Donald A. Ritchie, "1876," in Running for President, The Candidates and Their Images: 1789–1896, edited by Arthur M. Schlesinger, Jr.

the vote counts on the grounds that African Americans had been intimidated from going to the polls. One electoral vote in Oregon was also disputed. The system devised by the Founding Fathers for electing the president of the United States by electoral votes does allow for the possibility that the candidate with the majority of the popular votes may not be elected. But it does not

Campaign posters used the Centennial theme. Rutherford B. Hayes did not campaign but he encouraged his running mate, William A Wheeler, to do so. Wheeler declined, saying that crowds made his insomnia worse.
(Courtesy Collection of David J. and Janice L. Frent.)

Americans choose their presidents indirectly through what is known as the Electoral College system. The Framers of the Constitution conceived the system as a compromise between selection by Congress and election by direct popular vote. When citizens vote for a presidential candidate, they are in fact voting for a slate of electors pledged to that candidate. The winning electors in each state then cast their votes for president and vice president. A majority of electoral votes is needed to elect. In 1876, that number was 185 out of a total of 369.

provide for the possibility of contested electoral votes. Congress therefore established a special electoral commission to resolve the crisis. This was the first and only time in U.S. history that such a commission was used to settle a presidential election. The commission was composed of 15 men—5 U.S. senators, 5 members of the U.S. House of Representatives, and 5 justices of the Supreme Court. By a vote of 8 to 7, dividing along party lines with 8 Republicans voting for Hayes, all the disputed electoral votes went to Hayes, and he was declared the winner by a margin of one vote, 185 to 184.

THE COMPROMISE OF 1877. Some furious

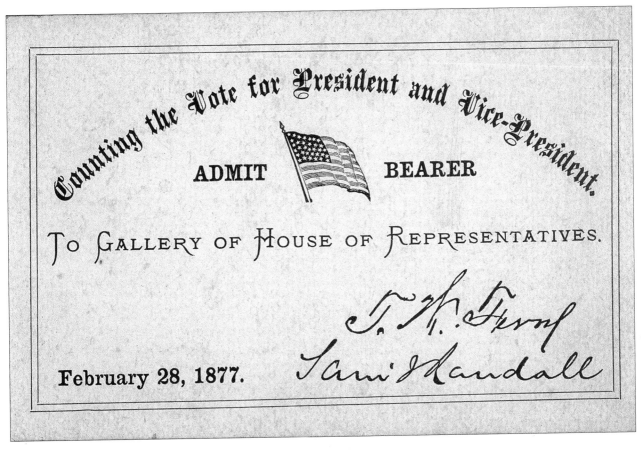

This is an admission ticket to the counting of the electoral votes in the U.S. House of Representatives. The presidential electoral votes were actually counted on 2 March 1877 at a joint session of Congress, but tickets with different dates had been printed in advance. (Courtesy Collection of David J. and Janice L. Frent)

Democrats threatened a rebellion because they felt that Tilden had been cheated out of the presidency. But Tilden gracefully accepted the results, calming the Democrats, who were further satisfied by Hayes's promise to withdraw federal troops from the South. This move ended the Reconstruction era and enabled white Democrats to reestablish their political control over the Southern states. This was called the Compromise of 1877. The political gains made by African Americans as a result of the Civil War and the passage of the Fourteenth and the Fifteenth Amendments were thereby taken away and made ineffective until the civil rights struggle rose in the decades following World War II. Hayes also promised to appoint a Southern Democrat to his cabinet, which he did with the appointment of David M. Key of Tennessee, as postmaster general. The Compromise of 1877 avoided a constitutional crisis, but it also meant that African American participa-

The "grandfather clause" was a provision in the constitutions of some Southern states that granted the right to vote only to those citizens whose fathers or grandfathers could vote before 1867. This meant that newly freed slaves, whose fathers and grandfathers had not able to vote, were also kept from voting.

This photograph of Rutherford B. Hayes was taken by Mathew Brady in his Washington gallery shortly before Hayes was inaugurated. (Courtesy Library of Congress)

INAUGURAL ADDRESS

. . . I ask the attention of the public to the paramount necessity of reform in our civil service—a reform not merely as to certain abuses and practices of so-called official patronage which have come to have the sanction of usage in the several departments of our government, but a change in the system of appointment itself; a reform that shall be thorough, radical, and complete; a return to the principles and practices of the founders of the government. They neither expected nor desired from public officers any partisan service. They meant that public officers should owe their whole service to the government and to the people. They meant that the officer should be secure in his tenure as long as his personal character remained untarnished and the performance of his duties satisfactory. They held that appointments to office were not to be made nor expected merely as rewards for partisan services, nor merely on the nomination of members of Congress, as being entitled in any respect to the control of such appointments.

The fact that both the great political parties of the country, in declaring their principles prior to the election, gave a prominent place to the subject of reform of our civil service, recognizing and strongly urging its necessity, in terms almost identical in their specific import with those I have here employed, must be accepted as a conclusive argument in behalf of these measures. It must be regarded as the expression of the united voice and will of the whole country upon this subject, and both political parties are virtually pledged to give it their unreserved support.

The president of the United States of necessity owes his election to office to the suffrage and zealous labors of a political party, the members of which cherish with ardor and regard as of essential importance the principles of their party organization; but he should strive to be always mindful of the fact that he serves his party best who serves the country best.

In furtherance of the reform we seek, and in other important respects a change of great importance, I recommend an amendment to the Constitution prescribing a term of six years for the presidential office and forbidding a reelection.

With respect to the financial condition of the country, I shall not attempt an extended history of the embarrassment and prostration which we have suffered during the past three years. The depression in all our varied commercial and manufacturing interests throughout the country, which began in September 1873, still continues. It is very gratifying, however, to be able to say that there are indications all around us of a coming change to prosperous times.

Upon the currency question, intimately connected, as it is, with this topic, I may be permitted to repeat here the statement made in my letter of acceptance, that in my judgment the feeling of uncertainty inseparable from an irredeemable paper currency, with its fluctuation of values, is one of the greatest obstacles to a return to prosperous times. The only safe paper currency is one which rests upon a coin basis and is at all times and promptly convertible into coin.

I adhere to the views heretofore expressed by me in favor of congressional legislation in behalf of an early resumption of specie payments, and I am satisfied not only that this is wise, but that the interests, as well as the public sentiment, of the country imperatively demand it. . . .

• *Rutherford B. Hayes delivered his Inaugural Address on 5 March 1877. He wanted to reform the civil service system to avoid corruption such as that which occurred during the Grant administration. Although both parties claimed to support this reform, Congress, controlled by the Democrats, did not act on Hayes's suggestions.*

THE RECONSTRUCTED SOUTH

. . . I suppose that here, as everywhere else, I am in the presence of men of both great political parties. I am speaking, also, in the presence of citizens of both races. I am quite sure that there are before me very many of the brave men who fought in the Confederate army: some, doubtless, of the men who fought in the Union army. And here we are, Republicans, Democrats, colored people, white people, Confederate soldiers, and Union soldiers, all of one mind and one heart today! And why should we not be? What is there to separate us longer? Without any fault of yours or any fault of mine, or of any one of this great audience, slavery existed in this country. It was in the Constitution of the country. The colored man was here, not by his voluntary action. It was the misfortune of his fathers that he was here. I think that it is safe to say that it was by the crime of our fathers that he was here. He was here, however, and we of the two sections differed about what should be done with him. . . .

What troubles our people at the North, what has troubled them, was that they feared that these colored people, who had been made freemen by the war, would not be safe in their rights and interests in the South unless it was by the interference of the general government. Many good people had that idea. I had given that matter some consideration, and now, my colored friends, who have thought, or who have been told, that I was turning my back upon the men whom I fought for, now, listen! After thinking over it, I believed that your rights and interests would be safer if this great mass of intelligent white men were let alone by the general government. And now, my colored friends, let me say another thing. We have been trying it for these six months, and, in my opinion in no six months since the war have there been so few outrages and invasions of your rights, nor you so secure in your rights, persons, and homes, as in the last six months. . . .

• *After his election, President Hayes toured the South, making speeches such as this one, delivered in Atlanta, Georgia on 24 September 1877. He had withdrawn federal troops from the South, and he trusted the state governments to protect the rights of the former slaves. He soon realized that he was fooling himself. African American citizens were not given their Constitutional rights.*

tion in the political process came to an end as Southern states quickly moved to take away the rights of African American voters by setting up a poll tax, promoting the grandfather clause as a voting requirement, and, above all, allowing the operations of white supremacy groups such as the Ku Klux Klan, which instilled fear into potential African American voters. Hayes had opposed slavery, but, as the Compromise of 1877 and his administration demonstrated, he was not a champion of racial equality.

The controversial legacy of the Compromise of 1877 overshadowed Hayes's one term in the White House. He faced a U.S. House of Representatives controlled by the Democrats. After the election of 1878, the U.S. Senate, too, had a Democratic majority. Hayes, an advocate of sound money, vetoed the inflationary Bland-Allison Silver Act (1878). Congress passed the bill over his veto, demonstrating the stalemate between Congress and the President.

Hayes supported civil service reform as a response to the corruption that had plagued the Grant administration, but Congress failed to act on his initiative. Hayes could only protest by issuing an executive order that barred government

This portrait of President Hayes hangs in the Rutherford B. Hayes Presidential Center in Fremont, Ohio. It was the first presidential library in the United States. (Courtesy The Rutherford B. Hayes Presidential Center, Fremont, Ohio)

employees from direct participation in political activities. Hayes did demonstrate his ability to take decisive action when he sent federal troops to stop riots that had broken out in several cities as a result of the nationwide 1877 railroad strikes. Another major divisive issue of the Hayes administration was the number of Chinese immigrants coming to California. Large numbers of Chinese laborers immigrated to the United States to work on the construction of the transcontinental railroads. By the early 1880s, they constituted almost 10 percent of California's population. While many in Congress sought to ban Chinese immigration altogether, Hayes vetoed the outright exclusion but compromised by limiting the number of Chinese who could enter the country. The Chinese Exclusion Act (1880) placed the first quota restriction on immigration in U.S. history.

RETIREMENT. When Hayes had won the Republican nomination for president in 1876, he had vowed that, if elected, he would serve only one term. In 1880, he honored that pledge. Hayes was a personally popular and well-liked president, but there were many in the Democratic Party who could never forget the manner in which he gained the presidency. Democrats felt that the election had been stolen from them, and in their national platform of 1880 they referred to Hayes's election as a great fraud that had weakened representative government in the United States. After leaving the presidency, Hayes retired to his home, Spiegel Grove, in Fremont, Ohio, from which he advised many Republican leaders. He became well known as an advocate for African American education, serving on the boards of the George Peabody Educational Fund and the John F. Slater Fund, both of which promoted African American education in the South. Hayes believed that education would ultimately heal the nation's racial problems. He also served as president of the National Prison Association, a prison reform group, and served as a trustee of several colleges and universities.

Lucy Hayes, who supported her husband in his charitable and civic-minded activities, died in June 1889. Her death was a severe blow to Hayes, but he continued to attend trustee meetings and work for the causes they represented. Hayes died on 17 January 1893. His home in Fremont, Ohio passed to the State of Ohio, and today it is the site of the Rutherford B. Hayes Library and Museum.

VICE PRESIDENT

William Almon Wheeler
(1819–1887)

CHRONOLOGICAL EVENTS

1819	Born, Malone, New York, 30 June
1846	Elected district attorney for Franklin County, New York
1850	Elected to New York State Assembly
1860	Elected to U.S. House of Representatives
1876	Elected vice president
1887	Died, Malone, New York, 4 June

BIOGRAPHY

The death of William A. Wheeler's father left his widow and small children in debt. In their upstate New York town of Malone, Wheeler's mother took in boarders to support her son's education. He attended the University of Vermont for two years until he dropped out due to eye trouble. Returning home, he taught school, studied law, and ran for local office as a Whig.

After serving as district attorney, Wheeler went to the state assembly and chaired the Ways and Means Committee. As a Republican, he was elected to the state senate and became its president pro tempore. He served one term in the U.S. House of Representatives during the Civil War and then chaired New York State's constitutional convention. In 1868, Wheeler won another term in the House and chaired the Pacific Railroads Committee. Although railroad lobbyists offered him stocks, he refused them, staying clear of the scandals that later damaged other members of Congress.

Wheeler gained national prominence during a House committee investigation of a disputed election in Louisiana in 1874. Going to Louisiana to examine the evidence, he devised a compromise that settled the dispute peacefully. The "Wheeler Compromise" also suggested a way to end federal Reconstruction of the South at a time when the North had grown weary of continuing the controversial program.

After the scandals of the Grant administration, Republicans in 1876 nominated a reform ticket headed by Ohio Governor Rutherford B. Hayes, with Wheeler as the vice presidential candidate. At the time of their nominations, Hayes had no idea who Wheeler was. During the campaign, Wheeler declined to make speeches because of his poor health. Because of a dispute over Southern electors, Hayes and Wheeler were elected by a special electoral commission.

When they finally met, Hayes and Wheeler enjoyed each other's company. A new widower with no children, Wheeler spent many evenings with the Hayes family at the White House. Hayes sought Wheeler's advice about patronage although not about policy.

A quiet, reserved man, Wheeler complained that he was excluded from both the President's cabinet meetings and from the Republican caucuses in Congress, and he was generally ignored by the press. When Hayes chose not to run for a second term, he thought Wheeler would make a good candidate to succeed him. Republicans instead turned to James A. Garfield. After losing a race for the U.S. Senate, Wheeler retired from public life.

THE CABINET

SECRETARY OF STATE
William M. Evarts, 1877

SECRETARY OF WAR
George W. McCrary, 1877
Alexander Ramsey, 1879

SECRETARY OF THE TREASURY
John Sherman, 1877

POSTMASTER GENERAL
David M. Key, 1877
Horace Maynard, 1880

ATTORNEY GENERAL
Charles Devens, 1877

SECRETARY OF THE NAVY
Richard W. Thompson, 1877
Nathan Goff, Jr., 1881

SECRETARY OF THE INTERIOR
Carl Schurz, 1877

President Hayes and his cabinet. Clockwise from left, Secretary of State William M. Evarts; Postmaster General David M. Key; Attorney General Charles Devens; Secretary of the Interior Carl Schurz; Secretary of the Navy Richard W. Thompson; Secretary of War George W. McCrary; Secretary of the Treasury John Sherman; and President Rutherford B. Hayes. (Courtesy Library of Congress.)

FAMILY

CHRONOLOGICAL EVENTS

28 August 1831	Lucy Ware Webb born	23 June 1858	Son, Rutherford Platt (Ruddy or Rud), born
30 December 1852	Lucy Ware Webb married Rutherford B. Hayes	2 September 1867	Daughter, Frances (Fanny), born
4 November 1853	Son, Sardis Birchard (Birch), born	8 February 1871	Son, Scott Russell, born
20 March 1856	Son, James Webb (Webb), born	17 January 1893	Rutherford B. Hayes died

(Courtesy Library of Congress.)

Lucy Ware Webb married Rutherford B. Hayes in her mother's home. As First Lady, she banned alcoholic beverages at the White House, earning her the nickname "Lemonade Lucy." She started the custom of an Easter egg roll on the lawn of the White House. She and the President also introduced the practice of singing hymns with the cabinet and congressmen on Sunday evenings.

A graduate of Wesleyan Women's College in Ohio, she was the first First Lady with a college degree.

Lucy Hayes lost three children in infancy but raised five others. At about the time her husband was inaugurated, Birch was graduating from Harvard Law School and setting up a practice in Ohio. Webb founded a business that grew into the very successful Union Carbide. He was awarded the Medal of Honor for his service in the Philippines during the Spanish-American War. He also started the Rutherford B. Hayes Library and Museum.

Rud graduated from Cornell. He worked for a bank in Ohio and worked very hard to promote libraries. Fanny married a naval officer who later taught at the U.S. Naval Academy at Annapolis. Scott was only six years old when his father became president. He became a businessman in New York.

PLACES

RUTHERFORD B. HAYES PRESIDENTIAL CENTER

1337 Hayes Avenue
Spiegel Grove
Fremont, Ohio 43420-2796
Tel: (419) 332-2081

*Rutherford B. Hayes died at
Spiegel Grove in 1893.* (Courtesy
The Rutherford B. Hayes Presidential
Center, Fremont, Ohio.)

*Located off the Ohio Turnpike at Exit 6. Once within the city, follow the signs for the Hayes Presidential
Center. Open Monday through Saturday from 9 A.M. to 5 P.M.; Sundays and holidays from 12 P.M. to 5 P.M.
Closed Thanksgiving, Christmas, and New Year's Day. Admission fee for the mansion and the museum,
with discounts available for groups and senior citizens. The Hayes Memorial Library and Museum and
the Hayes Tomb are located on the premises. The library is closed on Sundays and holidays. There is no
fee to use the library; donations welcome. The center is affiliated with the Ohio Historical Society.*

The site of Spiegel Grove, the home of President Hayes, was selected by his uncle, Sardis Birchard, a prominent businessman. Between 1859 and 1863, Birchard built the 25-room Victorian mansion and named it Spiegel after the German word for mirror to describe the reflecting pools of water in the grove. In 1873, Hayes made the 25-acre wooded estate his permanent home until his death in 1893. Hayes and his wife, Lucy, are buried on a wooded knoll near a section of the Sandusky-Scioto trail, a Native American trail which extends for half a mile through Spiegel Grove.

Three generations of the Hayes family lived on the property until it was given to the State of Ohio in 1910. Six years later, the Hayes Memorial Library and Museum was built on the estate. It was opened to the public on 30 May 1916. It was the first institution built specifically to house presidential papers and artifacts.

The museum contains more than 10,000 objects that belonged to Hayes, his family, and his administration, including his personal library and archival material from his military and political career. The library houses more than 1 million manuscripts and nearly 100,000 books, pamphlets and other material pertaining to Hayes and the Gilded Age (1860–1917).

◀ *Rutherford B. Hayes was the first president to have a library and museum created to house his presidential papers. The library now houses 75,000 volumes, and over 3,100 linear feet of manuscript and photographic material.* (Courtesy The Rutherford B. Hayes Presidential Center, Fremont, Ohio.)

Hayes's personal library included thousands of volumes of American history. They are now housed in the Hayes Memorial Library and Museum. This room appears as it did during Hayes's lifetime.
(Courtesy The Rutherford B. Hayes Presidential Center, Fremont, Ohio.) ▶

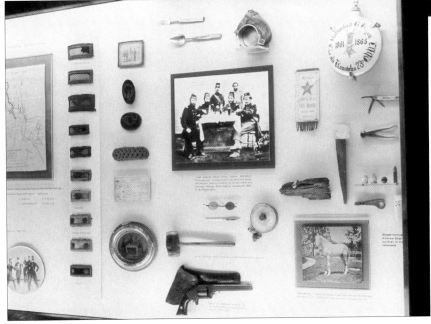

◀ *Equipment used by Hayes during the Civil War is on exhibit in the museum.* (Courtesy The Rutherford B. Hayes Presidential Center, Fremont, Ohio.)

James A. Garfield

20TH PRESIDENT
OF THE UNITED STATES OF AMERICA

CHRONOLOGICAL EVENTS

19 November 1831	Born, near Orange, Ohio
30 July 1856	Graduated from Williams College, Williamstown, Massachusetts
1859	Elected to Ohio State Senate
1860	Admitted to bar, Hiram, Ohio
21 August 1861	Commissioned lieutenant colonel in Ohio Forty-second Volunteer Infantry
10 January 1862	Promoted to brigadier general
7 April 1862	Commanded brigade at Shiloh
September 1862	Elected to U.S. House of Representatives
September 1863	Fought at Battle of Chickamauga
19 September 1863	Promoted to major general
5 December 1863	Resigned his commission in the U.S. Army
1866	Introduced bill to create a Department of Education
1871	Appointed chairman of House Committee on Appropriations
1876	Became House minority leader
13 January 1880	Elected to U.S. Senate; declined seat
2 November 1880	Elected president
4 March 1881	Inaugurated president
March 1881	Approved investigation of Star Route Frauds
2 July 1881	Shot by Charles J. Guiteau
19 September 1881	Died, Elberon, New Jersey

BIOGRAPHY

James A. Garfield was the second president of the United States to be assassinated and the last to claim birth in a log cabin. He was born on 19 November 1831 near Orange, Ohio, not far from Cleveland. His parents were farmers who lived along the Cuyahoga River. Garfield had three older siblings, two sisters and a brother. Garfield's father, Abram, died when Garfield was an infant, and his mother, Eliza, worked hard to keep the farm and to keep the family together. In 1842 she remarried, but after six years the marriage ended in divorce. Years later, Garfield would say his mother was the "molding agent" of his life. When he became president of the United States, she came to live in the White House.

As a boy, Garfield dreamed of going to sea. At age 16, he worked for a short time on a canal boat that made trips between Cleveland and Pittsburgh. He then resumed his education in local Ohio schools. In 1854, he entered Williams College in Massachusetts as a junior. There he was influenced by Mark Hopkins, a great teacher who was the president of Williams College. Garfield was so impressed with Hopkins that he would later say of him: "The ideal college is Mark Hopkins on one end of a log and a student on the other." Garfield graduated from Williams College with honors in 1856 and became an ordained minister and a professor of ancient languages at the Western Reserve Eclectic Institute (later Hiram College) in Hiram, Ohio. Before he was 30, Garfield was named president of this small school, which had a faculty of five. It was run by the Disciples of Christ (now the Christian Church). Garfield opposed slavery for religious reasons, and he joined the newly formed Republican Party. Elected to the Ohio State Senate in 1859, he resigned his seat to recruit the Forty-second Volunteer Infantry when the Civil War began. He was a large man and his energetic and friendly manner, combined with his skills as a public speaker and preacher, made him a popular figure in northeastern Ohio. Garfield campaigned for the Republican candidate, Abraham Lincoln, during the 1860 presidential campaign.

Although he had no prior military experience, Garfield was commissioned a colonel for the regiment he helped to form. He won promotion to major general in the Army of the Cumberland largely on the basis of his administrative skill and his bravery in the Battle of Chickamauga (1863).

When Garfield resigned his commission, he was chief of staff of the Army of the Cumberland under Major General William S. Rosecrans. (Courtesy National Archives.)

Garfield also ran for election to the U.S. House of Representatives in 1862, easily defeating his Democratic opponent. When Congress convened in December 1863, Garfield resigned from the army and took his seat in the House.

HOUSE OF REPRESENTATIVES. Garfield served in the House of Representatives for the next 17 years (1863–1880), resigning after being elected president of the United States. He also had been elected by the Ohio legislature to the U. S. Senate in 1880, an office he declined because of his election to the presidency. During his years as a congressman, Garfield's popularity with the other members of the House and his skill as a politician made him one of the most effective and respected members of the legislature. Garfield embodied many qualities that made him a popular national figure.

Like Abraham Lincoln, he was a self-made man who came from humble origins. He was a citizen soldier and a war hero. His personal style of casual friendliness and his lack of pretension made him popular even with his political opponents. He played a prominent role in the major events of the Reconstruction period after the Civil War. He rose to a leadership role in the House, serving on the Committee on Military Affairs in the last two years of the Civil War and later on two powerful committees that shaped much of Reconstruction policy, the Appropriations Committee and the Ways and Means Committee. Garfield would easily have been elected Speaker of the House, but the Republican Party lost its majority in the election of 1874. He was, however, his party's candidate for Speaker in 1875. During the last five years of his House service, he was the leader of the minority party. In 1877, Garfield served as a member of the Electoral Commission, created by act of Congress to examine the disputed presidential election of 1876 involving Samuel J. Tilden and Rutherford B. Hayes; Garfield voted in favor of Hayes. Garfield was one of the framers of the so-called Compromise of 1877, which settled the disputed election and also provided for the withdrawal of federal troops that had occupied the Southern states since 1865.

In 1880, Garfield's ambitions turned to the U.S. Senate and eventually to the presidency. One of the leading contenders for the Ohio State Senate seat and also a leading candidate for president was John Sherman, a former U.S. senator from Ohio who was secretary of the treasury during the presidency of Rutherford B. Hayes. Sherman sought Garfield's support for the presidential nomination and in return promised to support Garfield for the Senate. The bargain was kept, and Garfield was elected to the Senate by the Ohio state legislature. But in a surprising turn of events at the Republican National Convention, held in Chicago, Garfield, who started out to gain the presidential nomination for Sherman, ended up being the nominee himself. Garfield was able to outmaneuver Sherman's two chief opponents, James G. Blaine and Ulysses S. Grant, but still could not gain enough votes for Sherman to win the nomination. On the thirty-fifth ballot of the convention, part of the Wisconsin state delegation voted for Garfield. On the next ballot it was Garfield, not Sherman, who won the nomination. His vice presidential running mate was Chester A. Arthur of New York. In a reversal of the original plan, it was Sherman who returned to the Senate and Garfield who headed for the White House.

PRESIDENT. Garfield and Arthur won the presidential election with a plurality of close to 10,000 popular votes. His margin in the Electoral College was 214 to 155 over the Democratic ticket of Winfield Scott Hancock of Pennsylvania and William H. English of Indiana. The bland campaign was not one marked by major differences on the issues. The one issue on which the candidates disagreed was the tariffs on imported goods. Garfield supported high tariffs to protect U.S. manufacturers, while the Democrats supported a tariff only high enough to provide the necessary revenue to run the government. In his Inaugural Address on 4 March 1881, Garfield said: "The elevation of the Negro race from slavery to the full rights of citizenship is the most important political change we have known since the adoption of the Constitution in 1787." He made a strong appeal to the South to end

INAUGURAL ADDRESS

. . . The free enjoyment of equal suffrage is still in question, and a frank statement of the issue may aid its solution. It is alleged that in many communities Negro citizens are practically denied the freedom of the ballot. In so far as the truth of this allegation is admitted, it is answered that in many places honest local government is impossible if the mass of uneducated Negroes are allowed to vote. These are grave allegations. So far as the latter is true, it is the only palliation that can be offered for opposing the freedom of the ballot. Bad local government is certainly a great evil, which ought to be prevented; but to violate the freedom and sanctities of the suffrage is more than an evil. It is a crime which, if persisted in, will destroy the government itself. Suicide is not a remedy. If in other lands it be high treason to compass the death of a king, it shall be counted no less a crime here to strangle our sovereign power and stifle its voice. . . .

• *As early as 1881, President Garfield pointed out that guaranteeing the freedom to vote for all Americans was one of the most important things that government could do.*

President James A. Garfield (left) and Vice President Chester A. Arthur were pictured on the cover of the program for the 1881 Inaugural Ball. (Courtesy Collection of David J. and Janice L. Frent.)

its efforts to keep African Americans from voting and not to block their advancement as free citizens. One of the first things the new President tried to do in his brief term was to block the powerful New York political boss Roscoe Conkling and to end his control over important political posts in New York. President Garfield also faced a scandal within his own party that involved mail route contracts that were worth a lot of money (Star Route Scandal). Garfield ordered an investigation that blamed several top Republican officeholders, and, while there were no convictions, the investigation eventually led to important reforms in the civil service.

On the morning of 2 July 1881, while President Garfield was in a Washington, D.C. railroad station, he was shot twice by an assassin, Charles J. Guiteau, an insane man who had voted for Garfield. Guiteau claimed to be infuriated because he had been turned down for a government job. The President, despite several operations, never recovered and lingered bedridden until his death on 19 September 1881. His assassin was tried, convicted, and sentenced to hang for his crime. The sentence was carried out on 30 June 1882.

A great outpouring of national grief followed Garfield's death. Many biographies written shortly after Garfield's death praised his career as military hero, congressman, and president. A statue of Garfield stands in the Rotunda of the Capitol in Washington, D.C., and outside the Capitol, near the base of the west front of the Capitol grounds, stands a tall memorial statue of Garfield, a tribute to his many years of distinguished national service, especially in the U.S. House of Representatives.

▲ *This stained glass window was used as a sample by the manufacturer. It is an example of the grief felt by the country over Garfield's assassination.* (Courtesy Collection of David J. and Janice L. Frent.)

The memorial statue to Garfield stands on the United States Capitol Grounds at First Street, S.W. and Maryland Avenue. It was commissioned in 1884 by the Society of the Army of the Cumberland, of which Garfield had been a member. The statue was sculpted by John Quincy Adams Ward, a close friend of Garfield's. It was unveiled on 12 May 1887. It was incorporated into the Capitol Grounds in 1975.
(Courtesy Architect of the Capitol.) ▶

VICE PRESIDENT

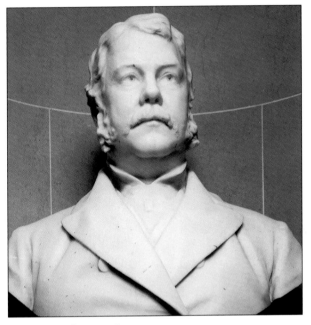

Chester Alan Arthur
(1830–1886)

CHRONOLOGICAL EVENTS

1830	Born, Fairfield, Vermont, 5 October
1848	Graduated from Union College, Schenectady, New York
1861	Appointed quartermaster general, New York State Militia
1871	Appointed collector of the Port of New York
1878	Removed as collector by President Rutherford B. Hayes
1880	Elected vice president
1881	Became president upon the death of James A. Garfield
1886	Died, New York, New York, 18 November

BIOGRAPHY

Son of a Baptist minister, Chester Arthur graduated Phi Beta Kappa from Union College and taught school before becoming a lawyer. During the Civil War, he served as quartermaster general of the New York militia.

Joining the political machine headed by New York Senator Roscoe Conkling, Arthur excelled as a party organizer and tactician. Thanks to Conkling's intervention, President Ulysses S. Grant appointed Arthur to the patronage-rich post of collector of the Port of New York. Grant's successor, the reform-minded Rutherford B. Hayes, ordered federal officials not to engage in political activities. When Arthur would not obey the order, Hayes fired him in 1878.

At the 1880 national Republican convention, Ohio Representative James A. Garfield was nominated for president. Seeking to unite the party by appeasing the powerful New York State delegation, Garfield's supporters offered Arthur the vice presidential nomination. Despite Conkling's sneers, Arthur could not bring himself to turn down the offer. Republican reformers were shocked over the nomination of someone as closely identified with machine politics as was "Chet" Arthur.

President Garfield depended heavily on Secretary of State James G. Blaine, Conkling's bitter rival. At Blaine's urging, Garfield appointed a political enemy of Conkling's to be collector of the Port of New York. Protesting the nomination, both New York Senators, Conkling and Thomas C. Platt, resigned from the Senate.

Vice President Arthur sided against the President and went to Albany to urge the state legislature to reelect Conkling and Platt. While he was there, on 2 July 1881, word came that President Garfield had been shot in Washington. The crazed assassin, who identified himself with Conkling's machine, had cried, "Arthur is president now!"

The assassination destroyed any chance of Conkling's reelection and banished him from politics. Shocked by Garfield's death, President Arthur reversed his earlier political position and endorsed civil service reform. He conducted himself in a dignified manner that helped him rise above his image as a party boss. Still, in 1884, Republicans denied him the nomination and gave it to Blaine, who was defeated. Having long suffered from kidney disease, Arthur died two years after leaving the presidency.

THE CABINET

SECRETARY OF STATE
James G. Blaine, 1881

SECRETARY OF WAR
Robert T. Lincoln, 1881

SECRETARY OF THE TREASURY
William Windom, 1881

POSTMASTER GENERAL
Thomas L. James, 1881

ATTORNEY GENERAL
Wayne MacVeagh, 1881

SECRETARY OF THE NAVY
William H. Hunt, 1881

SECRETARY OF THE INTERIOR
Samuel J. Kirkwood, 1881

(Courtesy Library of Congress.)

James G. Blaine (1830–1893). Blaine was appointed secretary of state by President James A. Garfield in 1881. He had previously served in the U.S. House of Representatives (1863–1875) and in the U.S. Senate (1876–1881).

As secretary of state, Blaine hoped to increase the influence of the United States in Latin America. He also sought U.S. control over the proposed canal in Central America. After Garfield's death in July 1881, Blaine agreed to serve briefly in the administration of Chester A. Arthur until a new appointment could be made. He retired in December 1881 to write the first volume of his memoirs, *Twenty Years in Congress.*

Blaine received the Republican presidential nomination in 1884. In the election of 1884, Blaine narrowly lost to Grover Cleveland. After the election, he retired to complete his memoirs.

In 1889, Blaine was appointed secretary of state by President Benjamin Harrison. He chaired the First Pan-American Conference in Washington, D.C. (1889–1890), and he managed to settle the dispute about seal hunting in the Bering Sea. He resigned in 1892 and died on 27 January 1893.

FAMILY

CHRONOLOGICAL EVENTS

19 April 1832	Lucretia (Crete) Rudolph born	17 January 1867	Daughter, Mary (Mollie), born
11 November 1858	Lucretia Rudolph married James A. Garfield	3 August 1870	Son, Irvin McDowell, born
		21 November 1872	Son, Abram, born
11 October 1863	Son, Harry Augustus, born	19 September 1881	James A. Garfield died
17 October 1865	Son, James Rudolph, born	14 March 1918	Lucretia Garfield died

The Garfield family did not enjoy the White House for long. President Garfield was sworn in on 4 March 1881, and he was shot by Charles J. Guiteau less than four months later. He died on 19 September 1881.

The books and the bookcase in this engraving show the interest that President and Mrs. Garfield had in education. They were both teachers at one time. All four sons followed their father in attending Williams College. Three of them went on to Columbia Law School and became lawyers. Harry became president of Williams College. James became secretary of the interior under President Theodore Roosevelt. Irvin became a successful businessman in Boston. The youngest, Abram, became an architect. Mollie was educated at private schools and married her father's secretary, Joseph Stanley Brown.

Eliza Ballou Garfield was the first mother to witness her son's inauguration. She was also the first mother of a president to live through the horror of her son's assassination. She had become a widow with four children when she was 31 years old. In spite of great poverty, she kept her family together. President Garfield's mother died on 21 January 1888, at the age of 86.

She is shown here wearing a cap and looking at her grandson, Abram. (Courtesy Library of Congress.)

PLACES

James A. Garfield National Historic Site, Lawnfield

8095 Mentor Avenue
Mentor, Ohio 44060
Tel: (216) 255-8722

It was from the porch of Lawnfield that Garfield launched one of the most successful front porch campaigns for the presidency. More than 17,000 people from all over the country came to hear him speak. A small, one-story building at the northeast corner of the house was used as the campaign office. (Courtesy The Western Reserve Historical Society, Cleveland, Ohio.)

Located on U.S. Route 20 in Mentor, Ohio, between Painesville and Willoughby, approximately 22 miles northeast of Cleveland. Take I-90 to the Route 306 exit. Open Tuesday through Saturday from 10 A.M. to 5 P.M.; Sunday from 12 P.M. to 4 P.M. Closed Thanksgiving, Christmas, New Year's Day, and Easter. Admission fee, with discounts available. Children ages 6 and under admitted free. Owned by the National Park Service, U.S. Department of the Interior, and operated by the Western Reserve Historical Society.

In 1876, James A. Garfield purchased Lawnfield, a rundown, one-and-a-half-story farmhouse on 118 acres of land. He lived there until his election to the presidency in 1880. In that same year, he added another story and a half to better accommodate his family and purchased 40 more acres of land.

In 1885, four years after Garfield's assassination, Lucretia, his widow, added a memorial library wing to the home using the donations she had received from the American people. The wing also housed third-floor bedrooms and a museum gift shop. It was the first presidential memorial library built in the United States.

Mrs. Garfield periodically lived at Lawnfield until her death in 1918. Surviving members of the Garfield family continued to live there until 1935, when the home was donated to the Western Reserve Historical Society. One year later, it was opened to the public. The furnishings include a waxed funeral wreath sent by Queen Victoria, Garfield's congressional desk, and the china used by the Garfields.

THE JAMES A. GARFIELD MONUMENT

Lake View Cemetery • 12316 Euclid Avenue • Cleveland, Ohio 44106 • Tel: (216) 421-2665

On 26 September 1881, President Garfield's funeral procession of more than 5,000 mourners made its way down Euclid Avenue in Cleveland, Ohio to the Lake View Cemetery, where he was entombed in a temporary vault. Nine years later, he was permanently entombed with his wife, Lucretia, in the James A. Garfield Monument. (Courtesy The Lake View Cemetery Association; photographer: Richard Kohl.) ▶

Located on the grounds of the Lake View Cemetery, situated near the edge of University Circle in Cleveland, Ohio. Entrances on 12316 Euclid Avenue and on Mayfield Road at Kenilworth. The cemetery is open daily all year, from 7:30 A.M. to 5:30 P.M. The monument is open daily during 1 April through 15 November only, from 7:30 A.M. to 5:30 P.M. Maintained and operated by the Lake View Cemetery Association.

The Garfield National Monument Association was formed within the weeks following the death of President Garfield. Its trustees announced a campaign to raise funds for the erection of a monument, and within two years $135,000 was collected. The Garfield family chose Cleveland as the place of entombment. Irish architect George H. Keller designed the monument, which was dedicated on Memorial Day, 1890. In 1923, the trustees of the association entrusted the monument to the Lake View Cemetery Association. An extensive renovation was completed in 1985.

The monument, a circular tower 50 feet in diameter and 180 feet high, is built of Ohio sandstone. The exterior is decorated with five panels that depict Garfield's life and death. The first four panels show a life-size figure of Garfield as teacher, statesman, soldier, and president. The fifth panel shows his body lying in state at the Capitol Rotunda in Washington, D.C. The interior contains a memorial hall featuring a marble statue of Garfield sculpted by Alexander Doyle. The statue is surrounded by mosaic walls and stained glass windows. The crypt that houses the bronze caskets of Garfield and his wife, Lucretia, is located directly below the hall.

◀ *Located within the memorial hall is the marble statue of Garfield sculpted by Alexander Doyle, who obtained the marble from the famed quarries near Carrara, Italy.* (Courtesy The Lake View Cemetery Association; photographer: Todd Williams.)

Chester A. Arthur

OF THE UNITED STATES OF AMERICA

CHRONOLOGICAL EVENTS

5 October 1829	Born, Fairfield, Vermont
1848	Graduated from Union College, Schenectady, New York
4 May 1854	Admitted to bar, New York
1 January 1861	Appointed engineer in chief of New York State militia
27 July 1862	Commissioned quartermaster general of New York State
20 November 1871	Appointed collector of Port of New York
11 July 1878	Suspended as collector of Port of New York
2 November 1880	Elected vice president
20 September 1881	Became president upon the death of James A. Garfield
4 April 1882	Vetoed Chinese Exclusion Act
1 August 1882	Vetoed Rivers and Harbors Act
16 January 1883	Signed Pendleton Act
1884	Did not receive nomination for election as president
18 November 1886	Died, New York, New York

BIOGRAPHY

EARLY LIFE AND CAREER. Chester Alan Arthur, the twenty-first president of the United States, was born on 5 October 1829 in Fairfield, Vermont. The youngest son of an Irish immigrant who became a Baptist minister, Arthur spent his boyhood moving with his family throughout the United States and Canada. Settling at last in New York, he graduated from Union College in Schenectady (1848), where he pursued a classical curriculum that emphasized Greek and Latin. For the next several years he made his living as a teacher while studying law. In 1852, Arthur traveled to New York City to work in a law office. In 1854, he was admitted to the New York State bar, beginning a notable legal career.

A strong abolitionist, he defended the rights of slaves in his two most noteworthy cases. In the first, he helped win freedom for eight slaves who were passing through New York while being transported by their masters from one slaveholding state to another. In the second, he won a test case that secured equal treatment for African Americans on streetcars and railroads in the city of New York. His antislavery sentiments led him from the collapsing Whig Party to the newborn Republican Party to which he became deeply committed.

Arthur was deeply involved in Republican politics both in New York and on the national level, and he participated in the Republican national convention

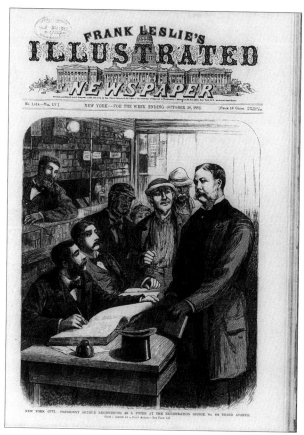

The cover of Frank Leslie's Illustrated Newspaper *of 28 October 1882 showed President Chester A. Arthur registering to vote in New York City which was his home from 1852 until his death in 1886.*
(Courtesy Library of Congress.)

in 1854. In 1856, he went to Kansas with a law partner, primarily to explore the profit potential of land speculation in that territory. The conflict he saw in "Bleeding Kansas" over the abolition issue strengthened his commitment to the antislavery, free-soil principles of the Republican Party.

After returning from this trip Arthur joined the New York State militia. When the Republican Edwin D. Morgan was elected governor of New York in 1860, he rewarded Arthur's loyal service to the party by commissioning the young attorney as engineer in chief of his general staff. This position required Arthur to wear a fancy uniform and accompany the governor on all state occasions. Arthur became friends with Morgan, the powerful governor of the most populous state in the Union and an important Republican leader.

It was during this period that Arthur courted and married a young woman named Ellen Herndon. Known as Nell, she was the daughter of a prominent naval officer and a society belle from Virginia. Arthur took over Mrs. Herndon's financial affairs when Captain Herndon died in a steamship disaster. Arthur married Nell soon after, in 1859. He compromised his abolitionist principles sufficiently to remain friendly with his wife's slaveholding Virginia relatives.

CIVIL WAR SERVICE AND POLITICAL CAREER. When the Civil War broke out in April 1861, Arthur's commission as engineer in chief of New York State became an important post. His rank was raised to brigadier general. Attached to the quartermaster general's office, he was responsible for feeding, clothing, housing, and equipping thousands of newly enlisted men assembling in the city of New York. Despite his lack of experience, Arthur performed this task with great skill and success. This duty, however, created tension between Arthur and his Southern-born wife. In 1863, he resigned his post and returned to his law practice.

Arthur spent the next several years amassing wealth and pursuing politics. His patron, Edwin Morgan, had been elected to the U. S. Senate, and Arthur aligned himself with Morgan's supporters in the New York Republican Party. Arthur became deeply involved in the Republican political machine in New York; he rose through a series of patronage appointments. In 1868, the Republican Civil War hero General Ulysses S. Grant was elected president. In 1871, Grant appointed Arthur to the moneymaking position of collector of customs for the Port of New York.

As collector he was responsible for collecting two thirds of the nation's tariff revenue, one of the principal sources of governmental income in the days before federal income taxes. He was a skillful administrator, supervising almost a thousand officials and running the customhouse with honesty and efficiency. In 1879, Grant's successor, President Rutherford B. Hayes, removed Arthur from the office in an act of civil service reform. By that time,

Arthur was the most prominent Republican in the city of New York. Arthur's hand guided most of the day-to-day operations of the Republican machine, led by Senator Roscoe Conkling, the political boss.

The dispensing of political jobs, both elective and appointive, by "bosses" was among the major activities of the machine. Essentially corrupt, this "spoils" system existed primarily for the benefit and enrichment of its participants, rather than for the good of the nation. In the decades after the Civil War, the enormous growth of industry and the number of government jobs created many new opportunities for corruption.

Grant had been so easy to manipulate as president that the spoils system came to be known as "Grantism." After four years of Hayes as president, the bosses of the Republican Party missed Grant. In 1880 this faction, known as "Stalwarts" and led by Conkling, sought to return the aging general to the White House for an unprecedented third term. This effort failed when the Republican National Convention, deadlocked between Grant and James G. Blaine, eventually compromised by nominating James A. Garfield for president. To unify the party for the coming election it was necessary to choose a Stalwart to run for vice president. Arthur, now chairman of the New York Republican Party, became that candidate.

ELECTION OF 1880. Months before the Republican National Convention, Arthur had suffered the greatest loss of his life when his wife Nell died suddenly of pneumonia at the age of 42. The coming election gave Arthur something important to concentrate on, and he threw himself into the presidential campaign. However, he admitted to a friend that he could no longer enjoy his triumphs as once he had without his wife to share them.

Arthur's candidacy met with immediate opposition from one of his oldest friends and patrons, Senator Roscoe Conkling. Conkling was by far the most forceful and influential member of the Stalwart faction. Still upset by his failure to get Grant nominated, he snubbed Arthur when Arthur had sought his approval on the convention floor a

short time later. Conkling was strongly tempted to withhold active support for Garfield and resisted having one of his underlings on the ticket. But Arthur made clear his intention to run with or without Conkling's blessing, and the Stalwart leader eventually accepted the situation.

Arthur's candidacy faced additional opposition from other groups within the Republican Party. Both the reformers and the "Half-Breeds," a rival group led by James G. Blaine, spoke out against him. Both groups opposed civil service reform, but they disagreed with each other's election strategy. Arthur was strongly criticized by the Democrats as well. He had never been elected to office and was regarded as the basic party hack. Nevertheless, Arthur became a major strategist of the Republican campaign, and his management was largely responsible for the victory that placed Garfield in the White House. They defeated the Democratic candidates Winfield S. Hancock and William H. English.

After Garfield's inauguration in March 1881, conflict arose immediately between the new President and the Stalwart faction. Arthur chose to side with his old cronies against President Garfield. The conflict was caused by Garfield's choice of Conkling's great rival, James G. Blaine, as secretary of state. Soon Garfield and Conkling were locked in a struggle to decide who controlled patronage in New York, a battle that resulted in the dramatic resignation from the Senate of both Conkling and Thomas Platt, the other New York Senator and a long-time Stalwart. Throughout the battle Arthur openly sided with the Stalwarts against the President. The issue was dramatically and decisively altered on 2 July 1881, when President Garfield was shot by Charles Guiteau, who declared himself a Stalwart and claimed he had acted to make Arthur president.

It was clear that Guiteau was insane and few believed that Arthur and Conkling had any involvement in the shooting. Still, there was widespread fear that, should Garfield die, Arthur as president would be little more than Conkling's

GEN. CHESTER A. ARTHUR.

REPUBLICAN CANDIDATE FOR VICE-PRESIDENT OF THE UNITED STATES.

NEW YORK, PUBLISHED BY CURRIER & IVES 115 NASSAU ST

When Chester A. Arthur received the Republican nomination for vice president, he had never run for elective office. He was a loyal party member and his choice was seen as a payoff to Roscoe Conkling, the New York political boss. (Courtesy Library of Congress.)

These cards were inserted into cigarette packages. They show the candidates in the election of 1880. (Courtesy Collection David J. and Janice L. Frent.)

tool. Many thought of Arthur as the worst sort of political creature, completely corrupt. Arthur himself was stunned and worried by the prospect of becoming president. That prospect became reality on 20 September 1881, when Garfield died, two months after he was shot.

PRESIDENT. The harsh assessment of Arthur by the press softened during the months that Garfield struggled for life. The Vice President had conducted himself well and had accepted the presidency humbly, promising to honor Garfield's memory by continuing his policies. His loyalties were still suspect, however, and as members of Garfield's cabinet began to resign, Arthur's appointments were closely examined. Several early appointments were longtime Stalwarts, but moderate, unobjectionable men. But then Secretary of State Blaine resigned. It was common knowledge that Conkling coveted the post and would relish this triumph over Blaine, his arch-rival.

This was a moment of truth for Arthur. If he appointed Conkling he would outrage a large segment of his own party, not to mention Democrats and the public at large. It would be an admission that he was Conkling's puppet. Instead, he chose Frederick T. Frelinghuysen, a prominent attorney

and a former senator from New Jersey. In this and other appointments he began to assert his independence from the political machine that had controlled his political life until then. The only Garfield appointee to remain in the cabinet until the end of Arthur's term was Robert T. Lincoln, the son of Abraham Lincoln.

The years of Arthur's administration were relatively uneventful. This accidental president was spared the ordeal of war, major foreign relations crises, struggles with major domestic issues, or economic catastrophe. Nevertheless, Arthur addressed a number of issues that would soon become very important.

Arthur used his veto power on several noteworthy occasions. For years there had been occasional disturbances against Chinese immigrants in the United States, reaching a peak during the depression years of the late 1870s, when inexpensive Chinese labor was felt to be a threat to American workers. In 1882, Congress passed the Chinese Exclusion Act which would have halted Chinese immigration for 20 years. While Arthur favored restrictions on Chinese immigration, Arthur felt that this bill was too harsh, and he vetoed the measure. This action received wide-

Veto of Chinese Exclusion Act

... The examination which I have made of the (1880) treaty and of the declarations which its negotiators have left on record of the meaning of its language leaves no doubt in my mind that neither contracting party in concluding the treaty of 1880 contemplated the passage of an act prohibiting immigration for twenty years, which is nearly a generation. . . . I regard this provision of the act as a breach of our national faith, and being unable to bring myself in harmony with the views of Congress on this vital point the honor of the country constrains me to return the action with this objection to its passage. . . .

I have said that good faith requires us to suspend the immigration of Chinese laborers for a less period than twenty years; I now add that good policy points in the same direction.

Our intercourse with China is of recent date. Our first treaty with that power is not yet forty years old. It is only since we acquired California and established a great seat of commerce on the Pacific that we may be said to have broken down the barriers which fenced in that ancient Monarchy. The Burlingame treaty naturally followed. Under the spirit which inspired it many thousand Chinese laborers came to the United States. No one can say that the country has not profited by their work. They were largely instrumental in constructing the railways which connect the Atlantic with the Pacific. The States of the Pacific Slope are full of evidences of their industry. Enterprises profitable alike to the capitalist and to the laborer of Caucasian origin would have lain dormant but for them. A time has now come when it is supposed that they are not needed, and when it is thought by Congress and by those most acquainted with the subject that it is best to try to get along without them. There may, however, be other sections of the country where this species of labor may be advantageously employed without interfering with the laborers of our own race. . . .

Experience has shown that the trade of the East is the key to national wealth and influence. The opening of China to the commerce of the whole world has benefited no section of it more than the States of our own Pacific Slope. The State of California, and its great maritime port especially, have reaped enormous advantages from this source. Blessed with an exceptional climate, enjoying an unrivaled harbor, with the riches of a great agricultural and mining State in its rear and the wealth of the whole Union pouring into it over its lines of railway, San Francisco has before it an incalculable future if our friendly and amicable relations with Asia remain undisturbed. It needs no argument to show that the policy which we now propose to adopt must have a direct tendency to repel Oriental nations from us and to drive their trade and commerce into more friendly lands. It may be that the great and paramount interest of protecting our labor from Asiatic competition may justify us in a permanent adoption of this policy; but it is wiser in the first place to make a shorter experiment, with a view hereafter of maintaining permanently only such features as time and experience may commend. . . .

• *In 1880, China agreed to a treaty giving the United States the right to "regulate, limit, or suspend" the immigration of Chinese laborers. This would modify the Burlingame Treaty of 1868 and it would be the first time that immigration from any particular country would be limited. Before 1882, immigration to the United States was free and unrestricted. In 1882, Congress passed a bill that would have kept Chinese laborers out of the United States for 20 years. This bill did not apply to teachers, students, tourists, or business persons, only laborers.*

Chester A. Arthur was sworn in by New York Supreme Court Justice John R. Brady at his home on Lexington Avenue in New York City at 2:15 A.M. on 20 September 1881. President Garfield had died several hours earlier. Arthur took a second oath at the Capitol in Washington, D.C. on 22 September. It was administered by Chief Justice Morrison R. Waite. (Courtesy Library of Congress.)

spread support from the press and from business interests eager to maintain friendly trade relations with China. Subsequently, Arthur signed a revised bill that became the Chinese Exclusion Law of 1882. It reduced the term of exclusion to 10 years but otherwise maintained the harsh restrictions of the previous bill. It was the first major limitation of U.S. open immigration policies.

Perhaps Arthur's most significant veto was of the Rivers and Harbors bill of 1882. This was a piece of popular "pork barrel" legislation that allowed members of Congress to secure appropriations for their districts. As sentiment against corruption grew, this legislation came to be seen by many as encouraging

fraud. Arthur's veto was hailed by the press, although Congress passed the bill over his veto. Nevertheless, the veto helped to establish Arthur's rejection of governmental corruption. It was a major step toward giving him a reputation for honesty and dedication to efficient government.

Since the end of the Grant presidency, groups in both the Republican and the Democratic parties had worked for civil service reform. The undeniable biases of the spoils system had been thrown into harsh relief by Guiteau's assassination of Garfield, since the assassin had felt himself wrongfully denied a patronage post, and Guiteau's self-identification with the Stalwarts shamed and

VETO OF RIVERS AND HARBORS ACT

. . . Many of the appropriations in the bill are clearly for the general welfare and most beneficent in their character. Two of the objects for which provision is made were by me considered so important that I felt it my duty to direct to them the attention of Congress. In my annual message in December last I urged the vital importance of legislation for the reclamation of the marshes and for the establishment of the harbor lines along the Potomac front. In April last, by special message, I recommended an appropriation for the improvement of the Mississippi River. It is not necessary that I say that when my signature would make the bill appropriating for these and other valuable national objects a law it is with great reluctance and only under a sense of duty that I withhold it.

My principle objection to the bill is that it contains appropriations for purposes not for the common defense or general welfare, and which do not promote commerce among the States. These provisions, on the contrary, are entirely for the benefit of the particular localities in which it is proposed to make the improvements. I regard such appropriation of the public money as beyond the powers given by the Constitution to Congress and the President.

I feel the more bound to withhold my signature from the bill because of the peculiar evils which manifestly result from this infraction of the Constitution. Appropriations of this nature, to be devoted purely to local objects, tend to an increase in number and in amount. As the citizens of one State find that money, to raise which they in common with the whole country are taxed, is to be expended for local improvements in another State, they demand similar benefits for themselves, and it is not unnatural that they should seek to indemnify themselves for such use of the public funds by securing appropriations for similar improvements in their own neighborhood. Thus as the bill becomes more objectionable it secures more support. This result is invariable and necessarily follows a neglect to observe the constitutional limitations imposed upon the lawmaking power. . . .

While feeling every disposition to leave to the Legislature the responsibility of determining what amount should be appropriated for the purposes of the bill, so long as the appropriations are confined to objects indicated by the grant of power, I can not escape the conclusion that, as a part of the lawmaking power of the Government, the duty devolves upon me to withhold my signature from a bill containing appropriations which in my opinion greatly exceed in amount the needs of the country for the present fiscal year. It being the usage to provide money for these purposes by annual appropriation bills, the President is in effect directed to expend so large an amount of money within so brief a period that the expenditure can not be made economically and advantageously. . . .

These objections could be removed and every constitutional purpose readily attained should Congress enact that one-half only of the aggregate amount provided for in the bill be appropriated for expenditure during the fiscal year, and that the sum so appropriated be expended only for such objects named in the bill as the Secretary of War, under the direction of the President, shall determine; provided that in no case shall the expenditure for any one purpose exceed the sum now designated by the bill for that purpose. . . .

• *On 1 August, President Arthur vetoed House bill 6242, titled "An act making appropriations for the construction, repair and preservation of certain works on rivers and harbors, and for other purposes."*

$11.4 million was appropriated for river and harbor improvements in 1881. The bill President Arthur vetoed appropriated $18.7 million. He felt that too much of that money was "for the benefit of the particular localities in which it is proposed to make the improvements."

embarrassed Arthur. When, in 1883, Congress passed the Pendleton Act (see page 38), the first national civil-service legislation, Arthur signed it into law. For the first time, some federal jobs would be filled by competitive exams rather than patronage. While this small step "classified" only 10 percent of federal jobs, it established an important precedent. The exam-based Civil Service would grow over the next decades to encompass all government positions.

FOREIGN POLICY. James G. Blaine was Arthur's secretary of state from March to December 1881. Blaine had taken an activist approach to foreign policy. He feared and resented the power of the British Empire and believed that Great Britain was constantly conspiring against the United States, its major trade rival. He was well aware of the new wave of European colonial expansion that had begun in the late 1870s and was especially concerned about British and French influence in Latin America. He was particularly worried about the War of the Pacific, that had broken out in 1879. The

---

DEDICATION OF THE WASHINGTON NATIONAL MONUMENT

Before the dawn of the century whose eventful years will soon have faded into the past—when death had but lately robbed this republic of its most beloved and illustrious citizen—the Congress of the United States pledged the faith of the nation that in this city, bearing his honored name and then as now the seat of the general government, a monument should be erected "to commemorate the great events of his military and political life." The stately column that stretches heavenward from the plain whereon we stand bears witness to all who behold it that the covenant which our fathers made their children have fulfilled.

In the completion of this great work of patriotic endeavor there is abundant cause for national rejoicing, for while this structure shall endure it shall be to all mankind a steadfast token of the affectionate and reverent regard in which this people continue to hold the memory of Washington. Well may he ever keep the foremost place in the hearts of his countrymen. The faith that never faltered; the wisdom that was broader and deeper than any learning taught in schools; the courage that shrank from no peril and was dismayed by no defeat; the loyalty that kept all selfish purpose subordinate to the demands of patriotism and honor; the sagacity that displayed itself in camp and cabinet alike, and above all that harmonious union of moral and intellectual qualities which has never found parallel among men—these are the attributes of character which the intelligent thought of this century ascribes to the grandest figure of the last. But other and more eloquent lips than mine will today rehearse to you the story of his noble life and its glorious achievements. To myself has been assigned a simpler and moral formal duty, in fulfillment of which I do now, as president of the United States and in behalf of the people, receive this monument from the hands of its builder and declare it dedicated from this time forth to the immortal name and memory of George Washington.

- *The Washington Monument, begun in 1848, was constantly delayed because of its cost. The original foundation sunk and had to be strengthened. "The present unfinished condition," declared President Hayes in 1877, "is a reproach to the nation." The final stone of the structure was laid in 1884. On 21 February 1885, President Arthur officially dedicated it to "The immortal name and memory of George Washington."*

  President Arthur made few speeches. He once said, "When I have anything to say to the country, I shall probably say it in black and white."

conflict was between Peru and Bolivia on one side and Chile on the other and the issue was control of nitrate mines in disputed territories. What bothered Blaine was the close ties between Chile and Great Britain, which had helped Chile develop the mines in territory leased from Bolivia. On

PENDLETON ACT

"Also known as the Civil Service Act, the Pendleton Act established the legal foundation for much federal personnel administration until it was superseded by the Civil Service Reform Act of 1978. The 1883 act was promoted by civil-service reformers, who became a political force in the 1870s and continued to exert influence until the 1890s, when they were overshadowed by the Progressive movement for more comprehensive governmental and economic reforms. The act substituted merit for partisan patronage as the basis for hiring federal employees in what became known as the competitive, or classified, civil service. The competitive civil service, which comprised about 10 percent of the federal service in 1883, eventually rose to about 90 percent. . . .

Specific provisions included (1) a Civil Service Commission with rule-making authority for personnel administration and administrative responsibilities for some aspects of federal personnel; (2) implementation of open, competitive, practical examinations for entrance into the classified service; and (3) development of rules to prevent partisanship in federal personnel administration. The act did not create significant legal barriers to the dismissal ofd federal employees."

• *David H. Rosenbloom, "Pendleton Act,"* The Encyclopedia of the United States Congress, *edited by Donald C. Bacon, Roger H. Davidson, and Morton Keller.*

Blaine's instructions, a series of inept U.S. diplomats attempted to influence the course of the war in favor of Peru, despite the fact that Peru was rapidly being overwhelmed by the Chileans.

The Arthur administration inherited these policies, but Arthur's new secretary of state, Frederick T. Frelinghuysen, had little taste for Blaine's brand of interventionism. While the failures of U.S. ministers to sway the combatants emphasized the need for a professional diplomatic corps instead of the amateurs appointed through the spoils system, the most compelling lesson of the war for the United States was its need for a strong navy.

The U.S. Navy had been allowed to fall into such disrepair after the Civil War that by 1880 it was reduced to a handful of old, poorly maintained wooden sailing vessels with auxiliary steam engines. The uselessness of this force as an instrument of foreign policy was proven when one of these ships was driven from a Chilean port by a modern Chilean ironclad warship.

Congress and the Arthur administration now agreed that not only were such established fleets as those of Great Britain and France threats to U.S. trade and security, but even minor Latin American powers had also become a danger. Arthur's secretary of the navy, William E. Chandler, strongly encouraged Congress to approve the construction of modern steel warships, and in March 1883, Arthur signed a bill into law appropriating funds for the first four ships of the modern U.S. Navy.

RETIREMENT AND DEATH. While Arthur's honest, careful stewardship of the presidency greatly improved his reputation and public esteem, there was little support for his reelection. He might have been able to force the issue of his nomination for the Republican presidential candidacy in 1884. However, by 1883 his failing health had convinced him that he was dying. He made few efforts on behalf of his own renomination, and the Republican convention chose his old foe, Blaine, as its nominee.

In the hard-fought election of 1884, the

Democrat Grover Cleveland narrowly defeated Blaine. Arthur played little role in the contest and was pleased to retire gracefully from office. He was widely hailed and praised for his honorable conduct as president.

Arthur returned to New York and a limited law practice. His health continued to fail, and he spent the last year of his life as an invalid. On 18 November 1886, he died of a massive cerebral hemorrhage. He was 57 years old.

Chester A. Arthur died at his home on Lexington Avenue in New York City on 18 November 1886. He had been sworn in as president there only five years earlier. (Courtesy Library of Congress.)

PRESIDENT CHESTER A. ARTHUR HISTORIC SITE

North Fairfield, Vermont 05455 • Tel: (802) 933-8362

The replica of Arthur's childhood home. (Courtesy The Vermont Division for Historic Preservation.)

Located approximately 3.5 miles east of Fairfield Station on the road that leads to State Route 108. Open Memorial Day through Columbus Day, Wednesday to Sunday, 10 A.M. to 4 P.M. No admission fee; donations welcome. For more information, write: Vermont Division for Historic Preservation, Montpelier, VT 05609-1201, or call: (802) 828-3226. Owned and maintained by the State of Vermont, Agency of Development and Community Affairs.

The President Chester A. Arthur Historic Site is a 1953 re-creation of the second house in which Arthur lived as an infant. A granite monument, dedicated in 1903, was situated on the small plot of land. At the time of its construction, the site was thought to be Arthur's birthplace, but that idea has long since been corrected. In 1950, the State of Vermont purchased the land around the monument and built the replica. An old photograph of the house that stood on the site was used as a guide. The actual building in which Arthur was born was a small cabin hastily erected in the village of Fairfield; the exact location is unknown.

▲ *The original home in which Arthur lived as an infant.*
(Courtesy The Vermont Division For Historic Preservation.)

President Chester A. Arthur was one of the two presidents born in Vermont. The second was Calvin Coolidge, the thirtieth president of the United States. (Courtesy The Vermont Division for Historic Preservation.) ▼

▲ *Arthur died in New London, Connecticut, and was buried next to his wife, Ellen, at the Arthur family plot in Albany, New York.* (Library of Congress.)

Grover Cleveland

22ND & 24TH PRESIDENT OF THE UNITED STATES OF AMERICA

CHRONOLOGICAL EVENTS

18 March 1837	Born, Caldwell, New Jersey
1859	Admitted to bar, Buffalo, New York
1870	Elected sheriff of Erie County
1881	Elected mayor of Buffalo, New York
7 November 1882	Elected governor of New York
4 November 1884	Elected president
4 March 1885	Inaugurated president
19 January 1886	Signed Presidential Succession Act
4 February 1887	Signed Interstate Commerce Commission Act
8 February 1887	Signed Dawes Severalty Act
11 February 1887	Vetoed Dependent Pension bill
2 March 1887	Signed Hatch Act
3 March 1887	Instituted repeal of Tenure of Office Act of 1867
6 November 1888	Defeated for reelection as president
March 1889	Returned to law practice in New York
8 November 1892	Again elected president
4 March 1893	Inaugurated president
9 March 1893	Withdrew Hawaiian annexation treaty from U.S. Senate
1 November 1893	Signed act which repealed Sherman Silver Purchase Act
28 June 1894	Signed Labor Day Act
3 July 1894	Sent federal troops to Chicago, Illinois to restore order during the Pullman strike
27 August 1894	Wilson-Gorman Tariff Act became law without his signature
1897	Retired to Princeton, New Jersey
1901	Appointed member of board of trustees, Princeton University
1904	Named president of board of trustees, Princeton University
24 June 1908	Died, Princeton, New Jersey

BIOGRAPHY

EARLY LIFE. Grover Cleveland, the twenty-second and twenty-fourth president of the United States, was the only president elected to two nonconsecutive terms. He was born on 18 March 1837 in Caldwell, New Jersey, the third of nine children of Richard Falley Cleveland, a Presbyterian minister, and his wife, Anna Neal Cleveland. Although the boy was named Stephen Grover Cleveland in honor of Reverend Stephen Grover, his father's predecessor at the Caldwell parsonage, the Stephen was never used.

When Cleveland was four years old, his father moved the family to Fayetteville, New York, near

Syracuse, where he became pastor of a local church. The Clevelands made several more moves within New York State during the next 12 years. Grover studied at local academies in Fayetteville and Clinton, another of his father's parsonages. At the age of 14, he worked as a clerk in a small store in Fayetteville, where he was paid $50 a year. His father died unexpectedly in 1853, three weeks after taking a new job in Holland Patent, a small village near Utica. Cleveland was 17 years old and had been preparing to enter Hamilton College, but his plans changed. He found it necessary from then on to earn his own living and help support his mother and his younger brothers and sisters.

His first job after his father's death was as a teacher at the New York Institute for the Blind, where his older brother William was principal. After a year of teaching, he decided to study law. On his way to Cleveland, Ohio, where he believed he would find work in a lawyer's office, he visited an uncle in Buffalo, New York. There he found a clerkship with a local law firm, Rogers, Bowe, and Rogers. Four years later, he was admitted to the bar. He spent three years working as an attorney for the firm.

Cleveland avoided serving in the Union forces during the Civil War by borrowing money to hire a substitute to take his place. In later years, he answered criticism from political opponents about this by claiming that he needed to take care of his mother. His two younger brothers had fought in the war.

ENTRY INTO PUBLIC LIFE. Cleveland began public service in 1863, when he was appointed assistant district attorney of Erie County. This brought him into close, regular contact with prominent local politicians, including former President Millard Fillmore, Fillmore's former postmaster general, Nathan K. Lane, and the powerful congressman Solomon G. Haven. While most of these men were Republicans, as indeed were most voters in Erie County, Cleveland was a loyal Democrat. When the district attorney died in 1865, Cleveland ran for the office. He was

defeated by the Republican candidate Lyman K. Bass, his close friend and future law partner.

Cleveland remained in private practice until 1870, when he was elected county sheriff, a job he held for three years. Returning to private practice, he formed a partnership with Lyman Bass and Wilson S. Bissell. He remained with this firm until 1881, when he ran for mayor of Buffalo. He was elected to that office by a wide margin.

As mayor, Cleveland gained a reputation as a reformer, using the power of the veto to override what he saw as corruption and graft. His initial veto prevented an appropriation of $500 from being used for the celebration of Independence Day instead of for Decoration Day, for which it had been designated. This, Cleveland maintained, violated an ordinance against using funds for purposes other than those for which they had been set aside. Later in his term as mayor, Cleveland vetoed a street cleaning contract that was awarded to one company even though a rival company had made a cheaper bid. In these and other instances, Cleveland used the power of his office to ensure what he saw as honest government. However, his reputation for honesty and integrity far exceeded his actual accomplishments.

Within a year of his election as mayor of Buffalo, Cleveland was chosen as the Democratic candidate for governor of New York. He was elected to that office in 1882. As governor he maintained the same style as he had as mayor of Buffalo—he continued to demand honesty, integrity, and efficiency and exercised his veto power unexpectedly. He called for and supported modest social programs such as supervision of banks, government involvement in public health and education, and the reform of municipal government. Unattached to political bosses, he earned the hostility of New York City's notoriously corrupt Tammany Hall, which increased Cleveland's reputation for trustworthiness. Perhaps most significant, his election as governor took him away from Erie County for the first time in nearly 30 years.

In 1874, Grover Cleveland fathered a child with a widow to whom he was not married. His opponents never let him forget it. A cartoon in a New York magazine in 1884 reminded readers of a popular saying of the day, "Ma, Ma, where's my Pa? Gone to the White House. Ha, Ha, Ha!" Although this created a large controversy in 1884, Cleveland was still elected president. (Courtesy Library of Congress.)

Cleveland's governorship also brought him to the attention of the national Democratic Party. The same qualities that had led to his being offered the nomination for governor suggested to the leaders of the party that the new governor of New York might make a very attractive national candidate. When, at the party convention in Chicago in the summer of 1884, the Democrats found themselves hopelessly divided among half a dozen worthy candidates, it became clear that Cleveland was the only man upon whom they could all agree. He was nominated for the presidency to great acclaim.

In the presidential election Cleveland adopted

An 1884 presidential campaign poster showed Grover Cleveland (top left) and Thomas A. Hendricks (top right). It recalled previous standard bearers and heroes of the Democratic Party: Thomas Jefferson holding the Declaration of Independence (bottom center); George McClellan (left); Andrew Jackson (right); and Samuel J. Tilden (top middle). (Courtesy Library of Congress.)

the unusual tactic of refusing to campaign. He made only two speeches during the entire election, both extremely short.

But the fate of his opponent, Republican James G. Blaine, was sealed when one of Blaine's most devoted supporters, the Reverend Samuel D. Burchard, called the Democrats the party of "rum, Romanism, and rebellion." Burchard made the remark in Blaine's presence. The uproar over this reference to old nativist fears of Catholic immigrants, to the alcohol consumption that Republican prohibitionists despised, and to

Democratic strength in the former Confederacy, greatly damaged Blaine's chances for election. Although Blaine disclaimed Burchard's words, they could not be taken back. It cost Blaine the crucial Irish Catholic vote in New York; New York had 36 electoral votes. Cleveland won, becoming the first Democratic president since 1860. In three years, Grover Cleveland had risen from mayor of Buffalo to the presidency of the United States.

PRESIDENT. Grover Cleveland entered the presidency at a relatively quiet moment in U.S. history. The great upheavals of the Civil War and

James G. Blaine and John A. Logan were the Republican candidates for president and vice president in 1884. Blaine was Speaker of the House, a U.S. senator, and served as secretary of state in the administrations of James A. Garfield, Chester A. Arthur, and Benjamin Harrison.

John A. Logan was a general in the Union army who was relieved by General William T. Sherman because of his involvement in politics. He was a member of the U.S. House of Representatives and a U.S. senator from Illinois. He conceived the idea of Memorial Day; it was formally observed in 1868.

They received 48.2 percent of the popular vote and 182 electoral votes; Grover Cleveland and Thomas A. Hendricks received 48.5 percent of the popular vote and 219 electoral votes. (Courtesy Collection of David J. and Janice L. Frent.)

Grover Cleveland was inaugurated for his first term on 4 March 1885. (Courtesy Library of Congress.)

Reconstruction were past. The Indian wars were largely over, trade and industry were growing, and "expansionism"— the empire building of the final decade of the nineteenth century and on into the early twentieth century, was still just an ill-defined dream in the minds of a small group of businessmen, politicians, and military officers.

Despite the relative quiet of the period, it was a transitional moment in the nation's history, and Cleveland's administration played an important role. The United States was changing from a rural, agricultural society to an urban, industrialized one. The makeup of the nation's population was being rapidly transformed as immigrants poured in from eastern Europe, Italy, and Asia. The nation had to decide what role government and the presidency should play in determining how the nation responded to these changes.

While Cleveland had a reputation as a reformer, this term would come to mean something quite different in a few short years. Cleveland stood for honest, impartial government and for fiscal conservatism, rather than for the great experiments of social engineering that would begin with the Progressives in the 1890s. Cleveland did not believe that government should be dedicated to the welfare of the people but only that it should seek to ensure "a fair field and no favor."

For a number of years a reform-minded branch of the Republican Party, known as Mugwumps, had been advocating an overhaul of the civil service so that government jobs would be given out on the basis of merit rather than patronage. Not only was this "more fair" than the spoils system; it would, they were certain, make government more efficient by placing the most competent people in administrative positions. Many Mugwumps had

voted for Cleveland, defecting from the Republican Party, and they expected the new President to reward them with dramatic civil service reform. They were disappointed when he failed to meet their expectations.

Cleveland recognized the need for change, but he also understood that the spoils system helped to ensure his own influence in his party. His approach was far more moderate than the

THE CEREMONY OF SUBMISSION.

Although Grover Cleveland had a reputation for honesty and integrity in government, his enemies portrayed him in political cartoons as bowing to the Tammany Tiger, the symbol for New York City's notoriously corrupt city hall. (Courtesy Library of Congress.)

FIRST ANNUAL MESSAGE

. . . Nothing more important than the present condition of our currency and coinage can claim your attention.

Since February, 1878, the government has, under the compulsory provisions of law, purchased silver bullion and coined the same at the rate of more than $2,000,000 every month. By this process up to the present date 215,759,431 silver dollars have been coined.

A reasonable appreciation of a delegation of power to the general government would limit its exercise, without express restrictive words, to the people's needs and the requirements of the public welfare.

Upon this theory the authority to "coin money" given to Congress by the Constitution, if it permits the purchase by the government of bullion for coinage in any event, does not justify such purchase and coinage to an extent beyond the amount needed for a sufficient circulating medium.

The desire to utilize the silver product of the country should not lead to a misuse or the perversion of this power.

The necessity for such an addition to the silver currency of the nation as is compelled by the silver-coinage act is negatived by the fact that up to the present time only about 50,000,000 of the silver dollars so coined have actually found their way into circulation, leaving more than 165,000,000 in the possession of the government, the custody of which has entailed a considerable expense for the construction of vaults for its deposit. Against this latter amount there are outstanding silver certificates amounting to about $93,000,000.

Every month two millions of gold in the public Treasury are paid out for two millions or more of silver dollars, to be added to the idle mass already accumulated.

If continued long enough, this operation will result in the substitution of silver for all the gold the government owns applicable to its general purposes. . . . The proportion of silver and its certificates received by the government will probably increase as time goes on, for the reason that the nearer the period approaches when it will be obliged to offer silver in payment of its obligations the greater inducement there will be to hoard gold against depreciation in the value of silver or for the purpose of speculating. . . .

The so-called debtor class, for whose benefit the continued compulsory coinage of silver is insisted upon, are not dishonest because they are in debt, and they should not be suspected of a desire to jeopardize the financial safety of the country in order that they may cancel their present debts by paying the same in depreciated dollars. Nor should it be forgotten that it is not the rich nor the money lender alone that must submit to such a readjustment, enforced by the government and their debtors. The pittance of the widow and the orphan and the incomes of helpless beneficiaries of all kinds would be disastrously reduced. The depositors in savings banks and in other institutions which hold in trust the savings of the poor, when their little accumulations are scaled down to meet the new order of things, would in their distress painfully realize the delusion of the promise made to them that plentiful money would improve their condition.

We have now on hand all the silver dollars necessary to supply the present needs of the people and to satisfy those who from sentiment wish to see them in circulation, and if their coinage is suspended they can be readily obtained by all who desire them. If the need of more is at any time apparent, their coinage may be renewed.

That disaster has not already overtaken us furnishes no proof that danger does not wait upon a continuation of the present silver coinage. We have been saved by the most careful management and unusual expedients, by a combination of fortunate conditions, and by a confident expectation that the course of the government in regard to silver coinage would be speedily changed by the action of Congress.

Prosperity hesitates upon our threshold because of the dangers and uncertainties surrounding this question. Capital timidly shrinks from trade, and investors are unwilling to take the chance of the questionable shape in which their money will be returned to them, while enterprise halts at a risk against which care and sagacious management do not protect.

As a necessary consequence, labor lacks employment and suffering and distress are visited upon a portion of our fellow citizens especially entitled to the careful consideration of those charged with the duties of legislation. No interest appeals to us so strongly for a safe and stable currency as the vast army of the unemployed.

I recommend the suspension of the compulsory coinage of silver dollars, directed by the law passed in February, 1878. . . .

- *It is hard to imagine how bitterly the country was divided during the 1880s and 1890s over the politics of money—whether to stay on a gold standard or to erode the value of the dollar by coining silver. Cleveland was a devoted "gold Democrat"—and for "sound money"—even though most Southern and Western Democrats supported the purchase and coining of silver to help the debt-ridden farmers.*

   In his First Annual Message to Congress, on 8 December 1885, the President pleaded for a repeal of the Bland-Allison Act (1878). This act, passed over President Rutherford B. Hayes's veto, required the Treasury to buy from $2 million to $4 million in silver a month and issue currency against it.

Mugwumps had hoped. While he carefully reviewed appointments himself—and he did ensure that far more positions were added to the "classified" list of jobs subject to merit evaluation rather than patronage—he considered the sweeping, radical reforms advocated by the Mugwumps to be impractical and unrealistic.

Within his own cabinet and the departments of government, significant reorganization was accomplished, particularly in the departments of the Treasury, the Interior, and the Navy. The Department of the Interior reorganized the Bureau of Indian Affairs in an attempt to ensure the rights of Native Americans and also tried to protect the rights of homesteaders against the claims of railroads and mining interests.

Cleveland was generally opposed to governmental interference in business affairs. However, he did recognize that some degree of federal regulation was needed to curb the greed and power of the railroads, the single most powerful industry of the day. He knew that the big railroad owners had received huge land grants and subsidies from the government to build transcontinental lines and then had failed to make good on their obligations to the government. He was also aware of railroad practices that forced communities to make enormous concessions to the rail companies or else be left off important routes, which could destroy them economically.

When the Supreme Court decided in 1886 *(Wabash v. Illinois)* that states did not have the power to regulate interstate commerce, Cleveland encouraged Congress to draft the Interstate

STATE OF THE UNION MESSAGE

. . . But our present tariff laws, the vicious, inequitable, and illogical source of unnecessary taxation, ought to be at once revised and amended. These laws, as their primary and plain effect, raise the price to consumers of all articles imported and subject to duty by precisely the sum paid for such duties. Thus the amount of the duty measures the tax paid by those who purchase for use these imported articles. Many of these things, however, are raised or manufactured in our own country, and the duties now levied upon foreign goods and products are called protection to these home manufactures, because they render it possible for those of our people who are manufacturers to make these taxed articles and sell them for a price equal to that demanded for the imported goods that have paid customs duty. So it happens that while comparatively a few use the imported articles, millions of our people, who never used and never saw any of the foreign products, purchase and use things of the same kind made in this country, and pay therefore nearly or quite the same enhanced price which the duty adds to the imported articles. Those who buy imports pay the duty charged thereon into the public Treasury, but the great majority of our citizens, who buy domestic articles of the same class, pay a sum at least approximately equal to this duty to the home manufacturer. This reference to the operation of our tariff laws is not made by way of instruction, but in order that we may be constantly reminded of the manner in which they impose a burden upon those who consume domestic products as well as those who consume imported articles, and thus create a tax upon all our people. . . .

But the reduction of taxation demanded should be so measured as not to necessitate or justify either the loss of employment by the working man or the lessening of his wages; and the profits still remaining to the manufacturer after a necessary readjustment should furnish no excuse for the sacrifice of the interests of his employees, either in their opportunity to work or in the diminution of their compensation. Nor can the worker in manufactures fail to understand that while a high tariff is claimed to be necessary to allow the payment of remunerative wages, it certainly results in a very large increase in the price of nearly all sorts of manufactures, which, in almost countless forms, he needs for the use of himself and his family. He receives at the desk of his employer his wages, and perhaps before he reaches his home is obliged, in a purchase for family use of an article which embraces his own labor, to return in the payment of the increase in price which the tariff permits the hard earned compensation of many days of toil.

The farmer and the agriculturist, who manufacture nothing, but who pay the increased price which the tariff imposes upon every agricultural implement, upon all he wears, and upon all he uses and owns, except the increase of his flocks and herds and such things as his husbandry produces from the soil, is invited to aid in maintaining the present situation; and he is told that a high duty on imported wool is necessary for the benefit to those who have sheep to shear, in order that the price of their wool may be increased. They, of course, are not reminded that the farmer who has no sheep is by this scheme obliged, in his purchases of clothing and woolen goods, to pay a tribute to his fellow farmer as well as to the manufacturer and merchant, nor is any mention made of the fact that the sheep owners themselves and their households must wear clothing and use other articles manufactured from the wool they sell at tariff prices, and thus as consumers must return their share of this increased price to the tradesman. . . . When it must be conceded that the increase of the cost of living caused by such tariff becomes a burden upon those with moderate means and the poor, the employed and unemployed, the sick and well, and the young and old, and that it constitutes a tax which with relentless grasp is fastened upon the clothing of every man, woman, and child in the land, reasons are suggested why the removal or reduction of this duty should be included in a revision of our tariff laws. . . .

The difficulty attending a wise and fair revision of our tariff laws is not underestimated. It will require on the part of Congress great labor and care, and especially a broad and national contemplation of the subject and a patriotic disregard of such local and selfish claims as are unreasonable and reckless of the welfare of the entire country.

Under our present laws more than 4,000 articles are subject to duty. Many of these do not in any way compete with our own manufactures, and many are hardly worth attention as subjects of revenue. A considerable reduction can be made in the aggregate by adding them to the free list. The taxation of luxuries presents no features of hardship; but the necessaries of life used and consumed by all the people, the duty upon which adds to the cost of living in every home, should be greatly cheapened. . . .

The simple and plain duty which we owe the people is to reduce taxation to the necessary expenses of a economical operation of the government and to restore to the business of the country the money which we hold in the Treasury through the perversion of governmental powers. These things can and should be done with safety to all our industries, without danger to the opportunity for remunerative labor which our workingmen need, and with benefit to them and all our people by cheapening their means of subsistence and increasing the measure of their comforts. . . .

• *President Cleveland devoted his entire 1887 State of the Union Message to the single subject of tariff reform. During the Civil War, tariff rates had been raised from an average of 19 percent in 1860 to over 40 percent in 1865. These high rates, supported by the Republican Party, were attacked by farmers—who sold their produce in a competitive market but bought manufactured goods in a market protected from foreign competition.*

Surplus funds piled up in the United States Treasury because of the revenue generated from these tariff acts. President Cleveland claimed that the surplus was a sign of overtaxation. In 1887, he called for lower tariffs. The tariff became the most important issue in the 1888 presidential election.

Commerce Act of 1887, which he signed into law. One of the first and most significant attempts at governmental regulation of business, the act created the Interstate Commerce Commission to investigate railroad business practices. While the act ultimately failed to control the railroads, it was an important first step in recognizing that there were times when government could not allow total freedom to business.

The U.S. Navy had been neglected for years after the Civil War. Under the Arthur administration that preceded Cleveland's, appropriations had been made for the navy's first modern warships in nearly two decades. Cleveland was convinced that a strong navy was essential to protect the United States from threats by European naval powers such as Great Britain and France. To defend U.S. trade and territorial interests, the Cleveland administration urged Congress to commission more new ships and encouraged industry to develop modern armor and naval guns.

Continuing the pattern he had begun as mayor of Buffalo and as governor of New York, Cleveland used his veto power unpredictably but to great effect. Always watchful against what he saw as the waste of government funds, he aroused the anger of Union veterans by vetoing scores of pension bills that he saw as fraudulent. He even vetoed the Dependent Pension bill, beloved by the veterans' organization, the Grand Army of the Republic (GAR). The bill would have provided a monthly pension to any veteran who claimed to be inca-pable of earning a living by physical labor. Calling the bill a public charity system, Cleveland cited its potential for fraud and enormous expense. With this veto he earned the undying hostility of the GAR, solidifying that organization's commitment to the Republican Party.

Cleveland made more enemies with his fiscal conservatism. In his first term the issue of "bimetallism"—the coining of currency on a two-

Allen G. Thurman was Grover Cleveland's running mate in 1888. Vice President Hendricks had died in office. Thurman had served in the U.S. House of Representatives and the U.S. Senate and was chief justice of the Supreme Court of Ohio. Cleveland and Thurman received more popular votes than the Republican candidates, Benjamin Harrison and Levi Morton, but they lost the vote in the Electoral College. (Courtesy Collection of David J. and Janice L. Frent.)

metal standard of gold and silver—began to gain importance. Cleveland was firmly opposed to placing more money in circulation by backing it with silver and was convinced that the gold standard was the basis for sound currency. He addressed this matter in his First Annual Message in 1885. While this was a heated issue during the economically prosperous 1880s, it would become absolutely dominant in the depression years of Cleveland's second term.

Finally, Cleveland's sense of fairness and financial conservatism led him to oppose protective tariffs. Believing that high tariffs aided trusts and increased the cost of living, Cleveland devoted his entire 1887 State of the Union message to tariff reduction. While his commitment to this issue angered monied interests, it helped solidify his image as a champion of fair play. In the election of 1888, he received the majority of the popular vote. However, due to the peculiarities of the Electoral College system, he was defeated by his Republican opponent, Benjamin Harrison, by a margin of 233 to 168. At age 51, Cleveland found himself out of office. He retired to practice law in New York and to enjoy the company of his new wife, Frances Folsom Cleveland, 27 years younger than him and the daughter of one of his former law partners.

Although Cleveland had left office determined not to seek it again, events of the next four years persuaded him that he was needed by his party and the nation. He feared the influence of "free silver" advocates in the Democratic Party and objected to expansionist tendencies among the Republicans. By 1891 he was actively seeking the Democratic nomination, and in 1892 he defeated President Benjamin Harrison after a dignified presidential campaign. Four years after his departure, Grover Cleveland found himself in the White House once again.

THE SILVER ISSUE. Cleveland and the Democrats had campaigned on the tariff issue, but the silver issue came to dominate his second term, and his response to the monetary crisis and the depression that compounded it undermined his reputation for years.

In the nineteenth century it was commonly assumed that currency was worthless unless there was something solid and valuable behind it. "Money" was either coins of precious metal, or paper currency that could be exchanged for "specie," gold or silver, upon demand. Throughout much of the century, most nations were on a "bimetal" standard, with gold and silver being coined at a fixed rate (although by the last decade of that century the world had largely followed Great Britain in adopting the "monometallic" gold standard). In the United States the exchange rate was around 16 to 1 through most of the century—16 ounces of silver was considered equal in value to one ounce of gold. This ratio, fixed by law, had little relationship to the commercial value fluctuations between the two metals.

The problem with this artificially established ratio was that changes in market value between the two metals affected their relative availability for coinage. For instance, after the Civil War the commercial value of silver rose, so silver producers could get more by selling their silver for manufacture into jewelry, silverware, and decorative items than they could by taking it to the U.S. Mint for conversion into coins and bullion. The amount of silver available to the government therefore diminished, and the government responded by producing more gold coin, virtually ceasing to produce silver coin. However, by the late 1870s there was so much silver on the market that the price of the metal began to drop, until its market value—what people would actually pay for it—fell to well below 16 to 1. On the open market an ounce of gold would buy as much as 30 ounces of silver. Worried silver producers therefore wanted to sell their silver to the government again, which was still offering a rate of 16 to 1.

In 1878, Congress passed the Bland-Allison Act to satisfy silver producers. The act required the government to purchase no more than $2 million to $4 million worth of silver per month to be

When Grover Cleveland was inaugurated on 4 March 1893, he became the only man to serve two non-consecutive terms as president. Vice President Adlai E. Stevenson was the grandfather of Adlai E. Stevenson II, the Democratic candidate for president in 1952 and 1956. (Courtesy Collection of David J. and Janice L. Frent.)

coined into silver dollars. This, combined with production of gold coin and limited amounts of paper money, became the government's currency output through the 1880s. But because the supply of gold was limited, by the late 1880s the amount of currency in circulation was insufficient to meet the demands of a rapidly growing economy.

As production rose, prices began to drop. The total amount of money in circulation is said to equal the total amount of goods available, and when the amount of goods increases while the money in circulation does not, then the same amount of money buys more and goods are worth less. The practical effect of this was that for producers like farmers, the value of their produce dropped, while their debts remained the same or grew. In fact, the gold supply was actually diminishing, as the government used gold to continue purchasing silver that it had no intention of coining. "Silverites" began demanding that the government increase the currency supply (the process known as inflation) by authorizing unlimited production of silver coin. This was the "free silver" issue, and its strongest supporters were the members of the

SECOND INAUGURAL ADDRESS

. . . Manifestly nothing is more vital to our supremacy as a nation and to the beneficent purposes of our government than a sound and stable currency. Its exposure to degradation should at once arouse to activity the most enlightened statesmanship, and the danger of depreciation in the purchasing power of the wages paid to toil should furnish the strongest incentive to prompt and conservative precaution.

In dealing with our present embarrassing situation as related to this subject we will be wise if we temper our confidence and faith in our national strength and resources with the frank concession that even these will not permit us to defy with impunity the inexorable laws of finance and trade. At the same time, in our efforts to adjust differences of opinion we should be free from intolerance or passion, and our judgments should be unmoved by alluring phrases and unvexed by selfish interests.

I am confident that such an approach to the subject will result in prudent and effective remedial legislation. In the meantime, so far as the executive branch of the government can intervene, none of the powers with which it is invested will be withheld when their exercise is deemed necessary to maintain our national credit or avert financial disaster. . . .

Under our scheme of government the waste of public money is a crime against the citizen, and the contempt of our people for economy and frugality in their personal affairs deplorably saps the strength and sturdiness of our national character.

It is plain dictate of honesty and good government that public expenditures should be limited by public necessity, and that this should be measured by the rules of strict economy; and it is equally clear that frugality among the people is the best guarantee of a contented and strong support of free institutions.

One mode of the misappropriation of public funds is avoided when appointments to office, instead of being the rewards of partisan activity, are awarded to those whose efficiency promises a fair return of work for the compensation paid to them. To secure the fitness and competency of appointees to office and remove from political action the demoralizing madness for spoils, civil-service reform has found a place in our public policy and laws. The benefits already gained through this instrumentality and the further usefulness it promises entitle it to the hearty support and encouragement of all who desire to see our public service well performed or who hope for the elevation of political sentiment and the purification of political methods. . . .

If we exact from unwilling minds acquiescence in the theory of an honest distribution of the fund of the governmental beneficence treasured up for all, we but insist upon a principle which underlies our free institutions. When we tear aside the delusions and misconceptions which have blinded our countrymen to their condition under vicious tariff laws, we but show them how far they have been led away from the paths of contentment and prosperity. When we proclaim that the necessity for revenue to support the government furnishes the only justification for taxing the people, we announce a truth so plain that its denial would seem to indicate the extent to which judgment may be influenced by familiarity with perversions of the taxing power. And when we seek to reinstate the self-confidence and business enterprise of our citizens by discrediting an abject dependence upon governmental favor, we strive to stimulate those elements of American character which support the hope of American achievement. . . .

• *Grover Cleveland was inaugurated for the second time on 4 March 1893. He was the only president to serve two nonconsecutive terms. The new invention of electric lights was featured at the Inaugural Ball.*

Populist Party. This new political party polled over a million votes in the 1892 presidential election and would have a major effect on the Democratic Party in 1896.

This approach seemed a path to disaster to fiscal conservatives like Cleveland. He entered office determined to solve the nation's monetary problems without resorting to the silverite solution. But before he could take any significant action the nation was plunged into crisis. Just two months after Cleveland's second inauguration came the panic of 1893—the beginning of the worst economic depression the nation had experienced to that time.

Cleveland began his second term by working for the repeal of the Sherman Silver Purchase Act of 1890, which threatened to pump huge quantities of silver coin into the economy. He feared that unlimited silver purchase and coinage would lead to increased hoarding of gold by private citizens, especially the wealthy. This would result in the United States adopting a single metal silver standard, which would severely damage U.S. foreign trade. Furthermore, inflation would hurt creditors, since the dollars paid back on loans would be worth less (have less purchasing power) than the dollars they had loaned. Since the passage of the Sherman Silver Purchase Act, the government had bought more than $147 million in silver, and gold reserves had dipped below $100 million. Worried creditors sought to redeem their paper and silver currency for gold, further draining supplies. While this issue was disturbing enough during prosperous times, it became extremely explosive when the economy collapsed.

THE PANIC OF 1893. The crisis began with the collapse of the Baring Bank in London, England. As other British banks bordered on collapse they demanded payment on loans to U.S. railroads. In March 1893, the Philadelphia and Reading Railroads, one of the largest U.S. railroads, declared bankruptcy. Two months later the bankruptcy of the National Cordage Company triggered a collapse of the stock market, followed by the failure of banks that had invested heavily in the market. As banks collapsed, it became difficult to get credit. Compounding these financial disasters was the drought that struck the Midwest in the early 1890s, destroying crops and financially ruining many farmers. The shock waves echoed throughout the economy as banks and businesses failed by the thousands.

To Cleveland the silver issue was at the heart of the economic depression. Public confidence in the economy was being destroyed by fears of unsound currency. The first order of business was the repeal of the Sherman Silver Purchase Act, which he pushed through Congress with all the powers available to the presidency. But keeping to the gold standard did little to reverse the depression, and Cleveland's dedication to monometallism turned virtually the entire agrarian branch of the Democratic Party, the "solid South" and the Midwest, against the President and his supporters.

Their anger was compounded in 1895, when the gold reserves dropped to $41 million. Fearing that the government itself would go bankrupt without a massive deposit of gold, Cleveland negotiated a loan deal with a small group of bankers led by J.P. Morgan. The bankers purchased $62 million worth of government bonds, paying half with gold from their own private reserves and the other half from foreign sources. Several more bond issues followed, leading to accusations that Cleveland was selling the country to big money interests. While these deals saved the government from bankruptcy, they did little to end the depression, which lasted well beyond the end of Cleveland's second term of office.

DOMESTIC FAILURES. His inability to reverse the depression was not the only failure of Grover Cleveland's second presidential term. Returning to the tariff issue, he personally helped draft the Wilson tariff bill, put before the House of Representatives at the end of 1893. Although the bill sought only modest tariff reform it emerged from the House in dramatically shortened and weakened form. The version finally sent to

PROCLAMATION: MARTIAL LAW IN CHICAGO

Whereas, by reason of unlawful obstructions, combinations, and assemblages of persons, it has become impracticable, in the judgment of the President, to enforce by the ordinary course of judicial proceedings the laws of the United States within the State of Illinois, and especially in the city of Chicago within said State; and

Whereas, for the purpose of enforcing the faithful execution of the laws of the United States and protecting its property and removing obstructions to the United States and protecting its property and removing obstructions to the United States mails in the State and city aforesaid, the President has employed a part of the military forces of the United States:

Now, therefore, I, Grover Cleveland, President of the United States, do hereby admonish all good citizens and all persons who may be or may come within the city and State aforesaid against aiding, countenancing, encouraging, or taking any part in such unlawful obstruction, combinations, and assemblages; and I hereby warn all persons engaged in or in any way connected with such unlawful obstructions, combinations, and assemblages to disperse and retire peaceably to their respective adobes on or before 12 o'clock noon on the 9th day of July instant.

Those who disregard this warning and persist in taking part with a riotous mob in forcibly resisting and obstructing the execution of the laws of the United States or interfering with the functions of the Government or destroying or attempting to destroy the property belonging to the United States or under its protections can not be regarded otherwise than as public enemies.

Troops employed against such a riotous mob will act with all the moderation and forbearance consistent with the accomplishment of the desired end, but the stern necessities that confront them will not with certainty permit discrimination between guilty participants and those who are mingled with them from curiosity and without criminal attempt. The only safe course, therefore, for those not actually unlawfully participating is to abide at their homes, or at least not to be found in the neighborhood of riotous assemblages.

While there will be no hesitation or vacillation in the decisive treatment of the guilty, this warning is especially intended to protect and save the innocent.

GROVER CLEVELAND

• *In 1894, the Pullman Palace Car Company lowered the wages of its employees an average of 25 percent. At the same time, it did not lower the rents and prices in the company stores in Pullman, Illinois. The company owned this town which was located just outside of Chicago.*

On 11 May 1894, over 2,000 employees quit and forced the closing of the stores. The local strike soon turned into a general railroad strike across the entire country. When two federal judges issued injunctions prohibiting all interference with trains, the workers ignored the orders and resorted to violence.

President Grover Cleveland sent federal troops to Chicago on 4 July. As a result, there was violence and rioting in cities throughout the country. However, the strike was broken, and Cleveland showed himself to be the enemy of labor.

Cleveland from the Senate was so drastically changed that Cleveland refused to either sign or veto it—a humiliating defeat for the President.

The depression increased tensions between business and labor that had simmered for decades, and in 1894 these tensions exploded in a workers' strike against the Pullman Palace Car Company, a major producer of rail cars. Previous labor actions such as the notorious 1892 strike against the Carnegie steel plant at Homestead, Pennsylvania, had been ended violently when state governors called out the National Guard. But when Illinois governor John Peter Altgeld refused to take action against the strikers, railroad bosses appealed directly to the President, who sent two thousand federal troops to break the strike. Cleveland had clearly labeled himself the enemies of organized labor by this action.

FOREIGN POLICY. Among Cleveland's rare triumphs in his second term was his handling of the Venezuelan Affair. When, in 1895, a border dispute between Great Britain and Venezuela over the British colony of Guiana threatened to escalate into open conflict, Cleveland intervened, citing concerns that British use of force would violate the Monroe Doctrine. The British responded that they did not consider themselves bound by the Monroe Doctrine. Angered by the British response, Cleveland and his secretary of state, Richard Olney, answered with a message so forceful and threatening that the startled British Government agreed to arbitration of the dispute by the United States.

Cleveland's response to the Hawaiian revolution had a far less decisive resolution. In January 1893, U.S. settlers under the leadership of the planter Sanford B. Dole overthrew the government of Queen Liliuokalani, with the assistance of marines from the U.S. Navy cruiser *Boston*. Confronted with the previous administration's intention of annexing Hawaii as a U.S. territory, Cleveland brought the process to a halt while he explored the issue.

In the years since Cleveland's earlier presidency, expansionist forces had grown very powerful, especially in the Republican Party. Influential men like Theodore Roosevelt and Senator Henry Cabot Lodge argued that the United States should build an overseas empire similar to the British. A great many politicians, businessmen, military officers, and ordinary citizens agreed. Grover Cleveland did not agree. Strongly anti-imperialist, the President was extremely concerned about U.S. involvement in the overthrow of the Hawaiian queen, and the reports of his investigator into the affair convinced him to reject the revolution. However, he submitted the problem to Congress rather than take action himself, thus ensuring that nothing would be done to reverse the takeover.

DEPARTURE FROM OFFICE. As a result of his handling of the silver question and the economic crisis, Cleveland had lost virtually all power in his own party by 1896. At the Democratic convention that year, the party rejected the President's policies and nominated William Jennings Bryan, a fiery young free silverite from Nebraska, as its candidate for the presidency.

Grover Cleveland was an extremely unpopular man when he retired from office. But national esteem grew for the former President, who lived quietly in Princeton, New Jersey. He served as a trustee of Princeton University and commented only rarely on public issues. In later years, he became associated with the insurance industry, which was happy to embrace his reputation for honesty and integrity. In the last year of his life, he served as chairman of the Executive Committee of the Association of Life Insurance Presidents. He died on 24 June 1908.

VICE PRESIDENT

**Thomas Andrews Hendricks
(1819–1885)**

CHRONOLOGICAL EVENTS

1819	Born, Zanesville, Ohio, 7 September
1841	Graduated from Hanover College, Indiana
1848	Elected to Indiana House of Representatives
1850	Elected to U.S. House of Representatives
1855	Appointed commissioner of the General Land Office
1862	Elected to U.S. Senate
1872	Elected governor of Indiana
1876	Ran unsuccessfully for vice president
1884	Elected vice president
1885	Died, Indianapolis, Indiana, 25 November

BIOGRAPHY

Born on an Ohio farm, Thomas A. Hendricks moved as a child to Indiana, where his uncle was elected governor. He graduated from Hanover College and studied law.

In the U.S. House of Representatives, Hendricks allied with Illinois Senator Stephen A. Douglas and voted for the Kansas-Nebraska Act. That vote cost him reelection in 1854, when he ran against an opponent supported by an antislavery coalition.

Hendricks's support for the Civil War made him a leading "War Democrat." When the U.S. Senate expelled Senator Jesse Bright as a Confederate sympathizer, the Indiana legislature elected Hendricks to fill the vacancy. One of only 10 Democratic senators, he often gave his support to President Abraham Lincoln.

Since those Democrats who opposed the war were discredited as "Copperheads," Hendricks became a potential presidential candidate in every election from 1868 until his death. He lost another race for governor of Indiana but finally won the office in 1872. Responding to the panic of 1873, Hendricks argued that impoverished farmers needed help. He advocated inflating the currency to reduce their debts. By contrast, Eastern financial interests supported the gold standard to protect creditors. At the Democratic National Convention in 1876, Easterners nominated New York Governor Samuel J. Tilden for president and then chose Hendricks to balance the ticket.

Although Democrats won the popular vote in the November election, the electoral votes of several Southern states were contested. A special electoral commission with a Republican majority gave the election to the Republicans. After the election, in 1884, Democrats chose him once again to run for vice president, this time with New York Governor Grover Cleveland. Hendricks campaigned vigorously and helped the Democrats win the presidency for the first time since the Civil War.

Vice President Hendricks opposed Cleveland's civil service reform efforts and demanded patronage for loyal Democrats. Known as the "Vice President of the Spoilsmen," Hendricks became a magnet for Democratic opponents of Cleveland. Whatever threat he might have posed for Cleveland ended when Hendricks died in his sleep while at home in Indianapolis.

VICE PRESIDENT

Adlai Ewing Stevenson
(1835–1914)

CHRONOLOGICAL EVENTS

1835	Born, Christian County, Kentucky, 23 October
1864	Elected district attorney
1874	Elected to U.S. House of Representatives
1878	Again elected to U.S. House of Representatives
1885	Appointed first assistant postmaster general
1892	Elected vice president
1900	Ran unsuccessfully for vice president
1914	Died, Bloomington, Illinois, 14 June

BIOGRAPHY

Born on a farm in Kentucky, Adlai Stevenson moved with his family to Bloomington, Illinois, where his father operated a sawmill. Working in the mill, Stevenson earned money to attend Centre College in Danville, Kentucky.

As a young lawyer, Stevenson entered politics as a Democrat. During the Civil War, he was elected district attorney. In the political and economic turmoil that followed the war, Stevenson won election to the U.S. House of Representatives in 1874, lost his seat in 1876, won it back in 1878, and was defeated again in 1880 and 1882.

When Grover Cleveland became the first Democratic president since the Civil War, he appointed Stevenson first assistant postmaster general. Earning the nickname "the Headsman" for his vigorous support of patronage, Stevenson fired almost 40,000 Republican postmasters and replaced them with Democrats. When Republicans returned to power, they in turn fired most of the Democratic postmasters.

As a reward for his party services, Democrats nominated Stevenson to run for vice president with Cleveland in 1892. Cleveland was a conservative, gold-standard advocate, while the more populist Stevenson supported free silver and currency inflation to help reduce farmers' debts. In 1893, President Cleveland called for repeal of the Sherman Silver Purchase Act. In their filibuster against the repeal, silver advocates were helped by Vice President Stevenson's rulings. Eventually, the U.S. Senate accepted a compromise that gradually reduced silver purchases over several years.

Stevenson enjoyed popularity on Capitol Hill because of his personality and his story-telling abilities. But he also attracted key free-silver supporters in Congress, who were known as the "Stevenson Cabinet." President Cleveland generally kept Stevenson uninformed, even when Cleveland secretly underwent cancer surgery. In 1896, Stevenson was a potential candidate to succeed Cleveland, but the Democratic nomination went to a young free-silver advocate, William Jennings Bryan. Bryan lost that election and ran again in 1900, with Stevenson as his running mate to add age and experience to the ticket. After their loss, Stevenson retired from politics. A half century later, his grandson and namesake, Adlai Stevenson II, would twice be the Democratic candidate for president.

THE CABINET

SECRETARY OF STATE
Thomas F. Bayard, 1885

SECRETARY OF WAR
William C. Endicott, 1885

SECRETARY OF THE TREASURY
Daniel Manning, 1885
Charles S. Fairchild, 1887

POSTMASTER GENERAL
William F. Vilas, 1885
Don M. Dickinson, 1888

ATTORNEY GENERAL
Augustus H. Garland, 1885

SECRETARY OF THE NAVY
William C. Whitney, 1885

SECRETARY OF THE INTERIOR
Lucius Q. C. Lamar, 1885
William F. Vilas, 1888

SECRETARY OF AGRICULTURE[1]
Norman J. Colman, 1889

1. Department of Agriculture established 15 May 1862.
On 8 February 1889, its commissioner was renamed
Secretary of Agriculture and became a member of the cabinet.

This fan shows President Grover Cleveland and his first cabinet around 1885. (Courtesy Collection of David J. and Janice L. Frent.)

(Clockwise, starting top left) Secretary of State Thomas F. Bayard later served as the first ambassador to Great Britain (previously representatives were called ministers); Secretary of the Treasury Daniel Manning died while in office in 1887; Secretary of the Interior Lucius Q.C. Lamar resigned to accept appointment to the Supreme Court; Attorney General Augustus H. Garland, Secretary of the Navy William C. Whitney, and Secretary of War William C. Endicott all served until 1889 and Postmaster General William F. Vilas was transferred to interior secretary in 1888.

THE CABINET

SECRETARY OF STATE
Walter Q. Gresham, 1893
Richard Olney, 1895

SECRETARY OF WAR
Daniel S. Lamont, 1893

SECRETARY OF THE TREASURY
John G. Carlisle, 1893

POSTMASTER GENERAL
Wilson S. Bissell, 1893
William L. Wilson, 1895

ATTORNEY GENERAL
Richard Olney, 1893
Judson Harmon, 1895

SECRETARY OF THE NAVY
Hilary A. Herbert, 1893

SECRETARY OF THE INTERIOR
Hoke Smith, 1893
David R. Francis, 1896

SECRETARY OF AGRICULTURE
Julius Sterling Morton, 1893

(Courtesy U.S. Naval Historical Center.)

Hilary A. Herbert (1834–1919). Herbert was appointed secretary of the navy by President Grover Cleveland in 1893. He had previously served as a representative from Alabama in the U.S. House of Representatives (1877–1893).

Herbert practiced law in Greenville, Alabama until the outbreak of the Civil War. He joined the Confederate army and rose to the rank of colonel. He fought in the battles of Fredericksburg, Antietam, and Gettysburg.

While in Congress, Herbert served as chairman of the committee on naval affairs and was largely responsible for the increased funding which led to the revival of the U.S. Navy. As secretary of the navy, he continued to work successfully for the expansion of the navy.

FAMILY

CHRONOLOGICAL EVENTS

21 July 1864	Frances Folsom born	28 October 1897	Son, Richard, born
2 June 1886	Frances Folsom married	18 July 1903	Son, Francis, born
	Grover Cleveland	1904	Daughter, Ruth, died
3 October 1891	Daughter, Ruth, born	24 June 1908	Grover Cleveland died
9 September 1893	Daughter, Esther, born	29 October 1947	Frances Cleveland died
7 July 1895	Daughter, Marion, born		

Frances Folsom was the daughter of Grover Cleveland's law partner. When her father died, Cleveland guided her education. In August 1885, shortly after her graduation from Wells College in Aurora, New York, Cleveland proposed to her in a letter. However, they did not announce their engagement until five days before their wedding. Cleveland, himself, wrote about 40 of their wedding invitations. Frances was 21 years old when she married President Cleveland, who was then 49 years old. She was the youngest First Lady and the first to marry a president in the White House.

Five years after the President's death, she married a professor of archaeology at Princeton University. She became the first presidential widow to remarry. During the Great Depression, she headed the Needlework Guild of America in its clothing drive for the poor. On 29 October 1947, she died in Baltimore, Maryland, and was buried next to the President at Princeton University.

(Courtesy Library of Congress.)

67

Former President and Mrs. Grover Cleveland were photographed at their home in Princeton, New Jersey with daughters, Esther and Marion and sons, Richard and Francis. (Courtesy Library of Congress.)

The Clevelands had three daughters and two sons. Ruth, their eldest daughter, was called Baby Ruth in the press and the candy bar was named after her. She died of diphtheria when she 12 years old. Esther, their second daughter, was born in the White House during Cleveland's second term. To date, she is the only child to be born in the White House. During World War I, she did volunteer work in England and married British Captain William Bosanquet. Marion, their youngest daughter, was born at their summer house in Buzzard's Bay, Massachusetts. She was community relations advisor for the Girl Scouts of America at its headquaters in New York from 1943 to 1960.

Richard, their eldest son, was born at Princeton University, when Cleveland was a lecturer and professor there. During World War I, he served as an officer in the U.S. Marine Corps. He graduated from Princeton University in 1919 and from Harvard Law School in 1924. He was an anti-New Deal Democrat and opposed the reelection of Franklin D. Roosevelt in 1936. Francis, their youngest child, was born in Buzzard's Bay, Massachusetts. Cleveland was 67 at the time of his birth. Francis studied drama at Harvard University and appeared in two Broadway shows, *Dead End* and *Our Town.*

PLACES

GROVER CLEVELAND BIRTHPLACE STATE HISTORIC SITE

207 Bloomfield Avenue • Caldwell, New Jersey 07006 • (201) 226-1810

Located at the intersection of Bloomfield and Arlington avenues in Essex County, approximately nine miles northwest of Newark. Open Wednesday through Friday from 9 A.M. to 12 P.M. and 1 P.M. to 6 P.M.; Saturday from 9 A.M. to 12 P.M. and 1 P.M. to 5 P.M.; Sunday from 1 P.M. to 6 P.M. No admission fee; donations welcome. The halls and doors can accommodate wheelchairs. Administered by the New Jersey Department of Environmental Protection, Division of Parks and Forestry.

Grover Cleveland was born on 18 March 1837 in the parsonage of the First Presbyterian Society of Horse Neck (now Caldwell), where his father, Reverend Richard F. Cleveland, was pastor. In 1841, when Cleveland was four, his family moved to Fayetteville, New York.

The birthplace was completed in 1832 at a cost of $1,490—at that time a large price for a house. It remained church property until 1913, when it was opened as a house museum by a private foundation. The site, a two-and-a-half-acre property, was acquired by the State of New Jersey in 1934.

Four rooms on the first level are open for viewing. They are furnished with President Cleveland's possessions, including his cradle, the top hat that he wore at his second inaugural parade, the family Bible, his fishing gear, and his marriage license. Many of the items were donated by his family.

On 18 March 1837, Grover Cleveland was born in the parsonage of the First Presbyterian Society of Horse Neck (now Caldwell), where his father was pastor. He was named after Reverend Stephen Grover, who had been the first minister of the Society 50 years earlier. (Courtesy Library of Congress.) ▼

◄ *Grover Cleveland died in Princeton, New Jersey, on 24 June 1908. Two days later, he was buried in Princeton Cemetery. Each year, on his birthday, a wreath from the White House is placed on his grave.* (Photograph by Charles E. Smith.)

Benjamin Harrison

23RD PRESIDENT
OF THE UNITED STATES OF AMERICA

CHRONOLOGICAL EVENTS

20 August 1833	Born, North Bend, Ohio
24 June 1852	Graduated from Miami University, Oxford, Ohio
1854	Admitted to bar, Cincinnati, Ohio
1856	Joined Republican Party
5 May 1857	Elected city attorney, Indianapolis, Indiana
1858	Appointed secretary of Republican state central committee
9 October 1860	Elected as reporter of decisions of Indiana Supreme Court
14 July 1862	Commissioned second lieutenant, Seventieth Indiana Infantry Regiment
23 January 1865	Promoted to brigadier general
10 October 1876	Defeated for election as governor of Indiana
28 June 1879	Appointed to Mississippi River Commission
18 January 1881	Elected to U.S. Senate
5 February 1887	Defeated for reelection to U.S. Senate
6 November 1888	Elected president
4 March 1889	Inaugurated president
2 May 1890	Signed act establishing Territory of Oklahoma
27 June 1890	Signed Dependent and Disability Pensions Act
2 July 1890	Signed Sherman Antitrust Act
14 July 1890	Signed Sherman Silver Purchase Act
6 October 1890	Signed McKinley Tariff Act
8 November 1892	Defeated for reelection as president
March 1893	Retired to Indianapolis, Indiana
1897	Published memoirs, *This Country of Ours*
1899	Served as counsel in Venezuela-Great Britain boundary dispute
24 November 1900	Appointed to Permanent Court of Arbitration, The Hague, Netherlands
13 March 1901	Died, Indianapolis, Indiana

BIOGRAPHY

Benjamin Harrison was born on 20 August 1833, in North Bend, Ohio. His family had been prominent in U.S. politics for a long time. His great-grandfather, also named Benjamin Harrison, was a signer of the Declaration of Independence. He was the grandson of William Henry Harrison, the ninth president of the United States. Harrison's father, John Scott Harrison, a prosperous Ohio farmer, served two terms in the U.S. House of Representatives (1853–1857). Harrison's mother, Elizabeth Irwin Harrison, died when he was still a teenager.

After three years of fighting in the Civil War, Benjamin Harrison returned to Indiana a war hero. He took part in the bloody battles of the Atlanta campaign. On 22 March 1865, he was brevetted (temporarily promoted) brigadier general "for ability and manifest energy and gallantry" in a citation signed by President Abraham Lincoln. Harrison is shown here (third from left) with other Union officers in a photograph taken by Mathew Brady. (Courtesy National Archives.)

EARLY CAREER. Harrison's education consisted of private tutors, attendance at a local one-room schoolhouse near North Bend, Ohio, and three years of college preparatory school in Cincinnati. He attended Miami University in Oxford, Ohio, where he excelled as a student of history and politics, graduating in 1852. While in college, he became known as an excellent public speaker who had a quick mind and could talk without preparation on a wide variety of subjects. But he also exhibited a stiff and formal style that later led some of his contemporaries to refer to him as the "human iceberg." He studied law at a Cincinnati firm, and he was admitted to the bar in 1854.

In 1853, he married Caroline Lavinia Scott of Oxford, Ohio, the daughter of a Presbyterian minister. In 1854, Harrison and his wife settled in Indianapolis. Later, as First Lady, Mrs. Harrison made it her personal project to oversee extensive remodeling in the White House, including the installation of electricity. She also conducted art classes in the White House.

In addition to practicing law in Indianapolis, Harrison joined the Republican Party in 1856 and became an active participant in party affairs in Indiana. He campaigned for John C. Frémont in 1856 and Abraham Lincoln in 1860. In 1861, as the Civil War began, he was serving an elected post as reporter of decisions of the Indiana Supreme Court. In 1862, Benjamin Harrison enlisted in the Seventieth Indiana Infantry Regiment as a second lieutenant. Before the Civil War ended he had risen to the rank of brigadier general. He served under General Joseph Hooker and General William Tecumseh Sherman in the Georgia campaign and was among the Union forces that took the city of Atlanta, Georgia, in 1864. After the war he returned to his law practice and to his job as reporter of decisions for the Indiana Supreme Court. In 1872, he sought the Republican nomination for governor of Indiana but failed to get the nomination. Some supporters in Indiana and Ohio thought Harrison should run for the presidency as early as 1876. Instead he

received the Republican nomination for governor of Indiana. He lost this election in a close race. Harrison continued to campaign actively for Republican presidential candidates, traveling throughout the East and the Midwest on behalf of Rutherford B. Hayes and, later, James A. Garfield. As a reward for Harrison's political support, President Hayes appointed him to the Mississippi River Commission in 1879.

In 1881, the Indiana state legislature elected Harrison to the U.S. Senate, where he served from 1881 to 1887. While in the Senate he was chairman of the Committee on Transportation Routes to the Seaboard from 1881 to 1883 and of the Committee on Territories from 1883 to 1887. Harrison became known as a good friend of Civil War veterans for his support of Civil War pensions. He was an early supporter of statehood for the Dakota Territory, but statehood was not achieved until 1889, two years after his term as senator ended. He also became an early champion of conservation, urging the preservation of land along the Colorado River. It would be another 20 years before Congress would begin to take up this issue with the establishment of the Grand Canyon National Monument and eventually Grand Canyon National Park. Harrison also followed the position of the Republican Party by supporting high tariffs. When it came time for the state legislature to renominate him for the Senate, in 1887, Indiana was in the hands of the Democratic Party, and Harrison lost the nomination. The following year he announced that he was running for the presidency.

ELECTION OF 1888. Harrison won the Republican nomination on the eighth ballot, over a field of six other candidates. The Republican platform for 1888 was not particularly surprising. It supported high tariffs, called for the reduction of some taxes, supported a strong navy and merchant marine, and urged reform of the civil service. The platform also added to this mix some of Harrison's favorite causes from his term in the Senate: increased pensions for veterans and statehood

This portrait of Benjamin Harrison was taken by Mathew Brady in Brady's studio in Washington, D.C. in the late 1870s. (Courtesy Library of Congress.)

WE ARE COMING, GROVER CLEVELAND

We are coming, Grover Cleveland
eight hundred thousand strong,
As vet'rans of the Union
to right our comrades' wrong,
Some now leave beds and crutches,
stout-hearted as of yore,
Your vetoes are behind us,
your insults are before,
Where Harrison is leading,
with shout and cheer and song,
We are coming, Grover Cleveland,
eight hundred thousand strong. . .

J.F. Watts, "Election of 1888," in Running for President, The Candidates and Their Images, *edited by Arthur M. Schlesinger, Jr.*

• *Neither Benjamin Harrison nor Grover Cleveland did much campaigning. However, their supporters were not above dirty politics. They produced a great deal of campaign material, often insulting in nature. This Republican song suggested that Union veterans of the Civil war would not vote for Cleveland because he vetoed their appeals for pensions. Also, Harrison was a veteran whereas Cleveland had never served in the army.*

for rapidly expanding western territories, such as Dakota. Another issue that was of growing concern at this time was how best to handle surplus money in the U.S. Treasury. The Republican platform called for reduction of taxes should the surplus grow. Harrison's running mate was Levi P. Morton of New York, a wealthy banker, who had served as minister to France from 1881 to 1885. The campaign was noted for its lack of controversy and for the low-key, polite manner in which both candidates conducted themselves. President Grover Cleveland did not actively campaign for reelection. He may have underestimated Harrison, his Republican rival. However, Harrison did little more, speaking only to the party faithful from his home in Indianapolis. Although others campaigned vigorously on their behalf, the two candidates themselves did not take to the campaign trail. The main policy difference between them centered on the issue of tariffs, with Cleveland supporting a lower tariff, but making it clear he was not in favor of completely free trade. Harrison supported a high tariff and protection for U.S. industry. In a very close contest with more than 11 million votes cast, Cleveland won the popular vote by about 100,000 votes, slightly more than one percent of the total vote. Cleveland failed to carry his home state of New York and Harrison won the electoral vote, 233 to 168. Local Democrats in New York state, part of the Tammany Hall machine that dominated New York politics for many years, opposed Cleveland, and their failure to support him cost him New York's 36 electoral votes.

This cotton bandanna highlights some of the policies favored by Benjamin Harrison and Levi P. Morton: protection of U.S. business (a high tariff), civil service reform, and reduction of the surplus money in the U.S. Treasury.

Bandannas such as this sold for about 10 cents in 1888 and the textile mills produced an uncountable amount of them. This particular item sells for about $500 today. (Courtesy Collection of David J. and Janice L. Frent.)

PRESIDENCY. During Harrison's term as president, he saw the fulfillment of his support for statehood of western territories with the admission of the new states of North and South Dakota, Montana, Washington, Idaho, and Wyoming. He was able to sign into law a new pension act, the Dependent and Disability Pensions Act of 1890, which extended benefits to more veterans and their dependents. During Harrison's presidency the first major antitrust legislation, the Sherman

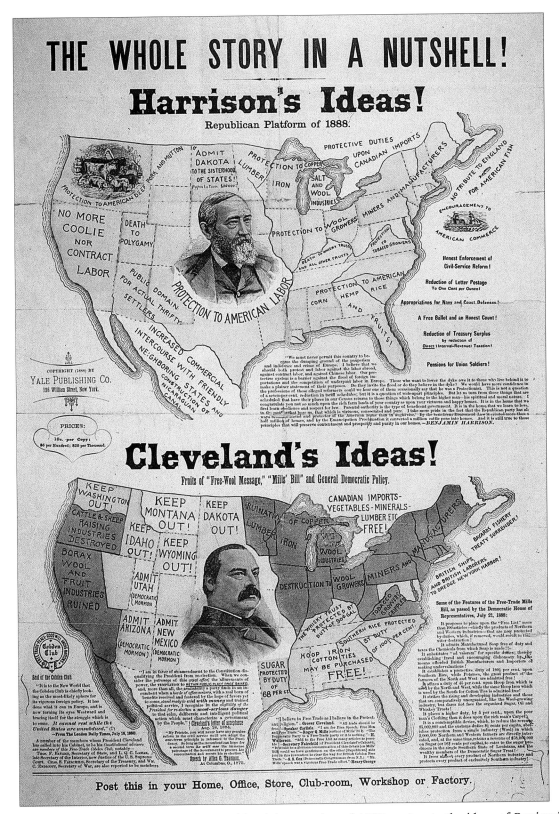

This print used by the Republicans in the presidential campaign of 1888 contrasts the ideas of Benjamin Harrison and Grover Cleveland. The major policy difference between the two candidates was the tariff. Harrison favored a high tariff and protection of U.S. industry. The tariff has not been a major policy issue since the end of World War II. The idea of protectionism has been replaced by mutual trade agreements.

(Courtesy Collection of David J. and Janice L. Frent.)

INAUGURAL ADDRESS

. . . The territory of Dakota has now a population greater than any of the original states (except Virginia) and greater than the aggregate of five of the smaller states in 1790. The center of population when our national capital was located was east of Baltimore, and it was argued by many well-informed persons that it would move eastward rather than westward; yet in 1880 it was found to be near Cincinnati, and the new census about to be taken will show another stride to the westward. That which was the body has come to be only the rich fringe of the nation's robe. But our growth has not been limited to territory, population and aggregate wealth, marvelous as it has been in each of those directions. The masses of our people are better fed, clothed, and housed than their fathers were. The facilities for popular education have been vastly enlarged and more generally diffused. . . .

If our great corporations would more scrupulously observe their legal limitations and duties, they would have less cause to complain of the unlawful limitations of their rights or of violent interference with their operations. The community that by concert, open or secret, among its citizens denies to a portion of its members their plain rights under the law has severed the only safe bond of social order and prosperity. The evil works from a bad center both ways. It demoralizes those who practice it and destroys the faith of those who suffer by it in the efficiency of the law as a safe protector. The man in whose breast that faith has been darkened is naturally the subject of dangerous and uncanny suggestions. Those who use unlawful methods, if moved by no higher motive than the selfishness that prompted them, may well stop and inquire what is to be the end of this. . . .

Our pension laws should give more adequate and discriminating relief to the Union soldiers and sailors and to their widows and orphans. Such occasions as this should remind us that we owe everything to their valor and sacrifice.

It is a subject of congratulation that there is a near prospect of the admission into the Union of the Dakotas and Montana and Washington territories. This act of justice has been unreasonably delayed in the case of some of them. The people who have settled these territories are intelligent, enterprising, and patriotic, and the accession of these new states will add strength to the nation. It is due to the settlers in the territories who have availed themselves of the invitations of our land laws to make homes upon the public domain that their titles should be speedily adjusted and their honest entries confirmed by patent. . . .

Let us exalt patriotism and moderate our party contentions. Let those who would die for the flag on the field of battle give a better proof of their patriotism and a higher glory to their country by promoting fraternity and justice. . . . We should hold our differing opinions in mutual respect, and, having submitted them to the arbitrament of the ballot, should accept an adverse judgment with the same respect that we would have demanded of our opponents if the decision had been in our favor.

No other people have a government more worthy of their respect and love or a land so magnificent in extent, so pleasant to look upon, and so full of generous suggestion to enterprise and labor. God has placed upon our head a diadem and has laid at our feet power and wealth beyond definition or calculation. But we must not forget that we take these gifts upon the condition that justice and mercy shall hold the reins of power and that the upward avenues of hope shall be free to all the people. . . .

• *Benjamin Harrison read his Inaugural Address on 4 March 1889 as Grover Cleveland held an umbrella over his head during a rainstorm. Harrison spoke of issues with which he was identified as a senator. Those issues were support of the Dakota Territory for statehood, high tariffs, and pensions for Civil War veterans.*

SECOND ANNUAL MESSAGE

. . . There is neither wisdom nor justice in the suggestion that the subject of tariff revision shall be again opened before this law [the McKinley Tariff] has had a fair trial. It is quite true that every tariff schedule is subject to objections. No bill was ever framed, I suppose, that in all of its rates and classifications had the full approval even of a party caucus. Such legislation is always and necessarily the product of compromise as to details, and the present law is no exception. But in its general scope and effect I think it will justify the support of those who believe that American legislation should conserve and defend American trade and the wages of American workmen.

The misinformation as to the terms of the act which has been so widely disseminated at home and abroad will be corrected by experience, and the evil auguries as to its results confounded by the market reports, the savings bank, international trade balances, and the general prosperity of our people. Already we begin to hear from abroad and from our customhouses that the prohibitory effect upon importations imputed to the act is not justified. The imports at the port of New York for the first three weeks of November were nearly 8 percent greater than for the same period in 1889 and 29 percent greater than in the same period of 1888. And so far from being an act to limit exports, I confidently believe that under it we shall secure a larger and more profitable participation in foreign trade than we have ever enjoyed, and that we shall recover a proportionate participation in the ocean carrying trade of the world.

The criticisms of the bill that have come to us from foreign sources may well be rejected for repugnancy. If these critics really believe that the adoption by us of a free-trade policy, or of tariff rates having reference solely to revenue, would diminish the participation of their own countries in the commerce of the world, their advocacy and promotion, by speech and other forms of organized effort, of this movement among our people is a rare exhibition of unselfishness in trade. And, on the other hand, if they sincerely believe that the adoption of a protective tariff policy by this country inures to their profit and our hurt, it is noticeably strange that they should lead the outcry against the authors of a policy so helpful to their countrymen and crown with their favor those who would snatch from them a substantial share of a trade with other hands already inadequate to their necessities. . . .

From the time of my induction into office the duty of using every power and influence given by law to the executive department for the development of larger markets for our products, especially our farm products, has been kept constantly in mind, and no effort has been or will be spared to promote that end. We are under no disadvantage in any foreign market, except that we pay our workmen and workwomen better wages than are paid elsewhere—better abstractly, better relatively to the cost of the necessaries of life. I do not doubt that a very largely increased foreign trade is accessible to us without bartering for it either our home market for such products of the farm and shop as our own people can supply or the wages of our working people. . . .

- *President Benjamin Harrison delivered his Second Annual Message to Congress on 1 December 1890. A large part of it discussed the new McKinley Tariff. He expected this new tariff to protect U.S. workers and discourage foreign competition.*

An advertising card from a manufacturing firm shows the presidential and vice presidential candidates of the Democratic and Republican parties in 1892. Whitelaw Reid, Harrison's running mate, was publisher of the New York Tribune *and minister to France.* (Courtesy Collection of David J. and Janice L. Frent.)

Antitrust Act of 1890, called attention to the growing problem of monopolies and the ways in which they undermined commerce and stifled competition. Also in 1890, Congress passed and the President signed major tariff legislation and a bill to guarantee the purchase of large amounts of western silver.

The McKinley Tariff Act (named for Representative William McKinley) raised the tariff to new peacetime highs, resulting in sharp increases in the prices of many consumer goods. The public reaction to the higher prices was to elect more Democrats to Congress in 1890. Two years later, in the presidential election of 1892, the country was ready to return to Grover Cleveland and a lower tariff. The presidential campaign of 1892 was as dull as the one in 1888. This time around, however, both the Republican and the Democratic candidates could claim experience, having each served a term as president. Unfortunately, just weeks before the election Harrison's wife, Caroline, died. Both candidates stopped campaigning. Some observers thought that Harrison lost interest in the campaign and the presidency after the death of his wife. As it had been in 1888, the major issue in the campaign was the tariff. Additional interest in the campaign was generated by the candidate of the People's Party, James B. Weaver. Weaver called for the free coinage of silver, a policy popular in the new western states, where the silver was mined. Weaver managed to attract 9 percent of the popular vote and won 22 electoral votes, all from western states. But this time around Cleveland defeated Harrison by almost 400,000 popular votes and won in the Electoral College, 277 to 145.

RETIREMENT. Harrison attended his successor's inauguration on 4 March 1893 and then retired to an active life as a lawyer, writer, and public speaker. For two years, from 1897 to 1899, he was counsel for Venezuela in that country's boundary dispute with Great Britain. He wrote two books in the years following his presidency, *This Country of Ours* (1897) and *Views of an Ex-President* (1901). In 1896, Harrison married again. This time he wed a young widow, Mary Scott Lord Dimmick, who was his first wife's niece. On 13 March 1901, Harrison died of pneumonia; he was buried in Indianapolis, Indiana.

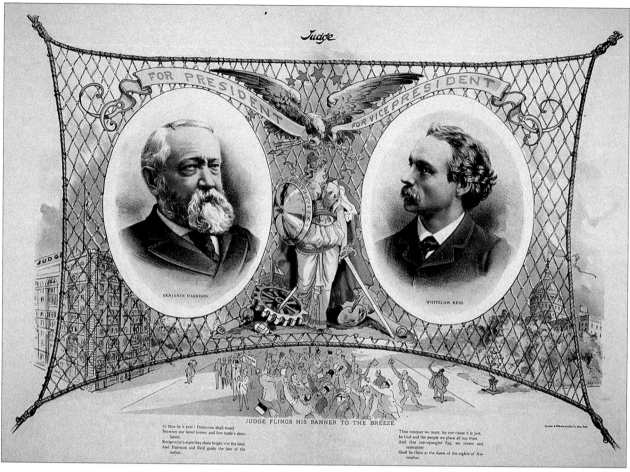

(Courtesy Collection of David J. and Janice L. Frent.)

This is the centerfold from Judge, *a weekly Republican magazine. The text at the bottom was intended to be sung to the music of The Star-Spangled Banner. It stresses the importance of the tariff supported by Harrison and the Republicans. The date in the last line was election day in 1892.*

O, thus be it ever! Protection shall stand
Between our loved homes and free trade's desolation.
Reciprocity's stars they shine bright o'er the land,
And Harrison and Reid guide the fate of the nation.

Thus conquer we must, for our cause it is just.
In God and the people we place all our trust,
And that star-spangled flag we revere and remember
Shall be there at the dawn of the eighth of November.

VICE PRESIDENT

Levi Parsons Morton
(1824–1920)

CHRONOLOGICAL EVENTS

1824	Born, Shoreham, Vermont, 16 May
1878	Elected to U.S. House of Representatives
1881	Appointed U.S. minister to France
1888	Elected vice president
1894	Elected governor of New York
1920	Died, Rhinebeck, New York, 16 May

BIOGRAPHY

Although he later became one of the nation's richest men, Levi P. Morton was unable to go to college because his father, a Congregational minister, could not afford the expense. Morton instead clerked at a general store, where he learned bookkeeping. When the store went bankrupt, its chief creditor was so impressed with the young clerk that he hired him for his importing business in Boston. In 1854, the company sent Morton to its office in New York. Morton soon established his own company to import Southern cotton for New England's textile mills. The Civil War ended that business, and Morton founded a Wall Street bank, Morton, Bliss & Company. Within a few years he had become one of the nation's most prominent bankers.

President Ulysses S. Grant used Morton's bank to handle the federal government's international transactions. In 1876, Morton became financial chairman of the Republican National Committee and also narrowly lost an election to the U.S. House of Representatives. He won the seat in 1878.

Republicans nominated James A. Garfield for president in 1880 and offered the vice presidential nomination to Morton to help carry New York. But the leader of the New York delegation, Senator Roscoe Conkling, persuaded Morton to decline. The nomination went instead to Chester A. Arthur, who became president following Garfield's assassination.

Appointed U.S. minister to France, Morton helped bring the Statue of Liberty to New York Harbor. Twice he ran unsuccessfully for senator. Finally, in 1888, Morton accepted the vice presidential nomination with Indiana Senator Benjamin Harrison. They lost the popular vote but won the election in the Electoral College.

Vice President Morton fit comfortably into an administration dominated by wealthy businessmen, but he disappointed Harrison by his performance in the U.S. Senate. Harrison had called on Senate Republicans to pass a "force bill" to protect African American voters in the South. Morton cast the tie-breaking vote to bring the bill to the Senate floor. Yet he declined to make any ruling that might break the Southern filibuster that eventually killed the bill.

Without Harrison's support, Morton was replaced on the Republican ticket in 1892 by Whitelaw Reid, the editor of the *New York Tribune*. Two years later, Morton won election as governor of New York and was New York's "favorite son" candidate for president in 1896. Defeated by William McKinley, he returned to banking. In 1909, Morton's bank merged with J.P. Morgan's to form the Morgan Guaranty Trust Company, and his name faded from both banking and politics.

THE CABINET

SECRETARY OF STATE
James G. Blaine, 1889
John W. Foster, 1892

SECRETARY OF WAR
Redfield Proctor, 1889
Stephen B. Elkins, 1891

SECRETARY OF THE TREASURY
William Windom, 1889
Charles Foster, 1891

POSTMASTER GENERAL
John Wanamaker, 1889

ATTORNEY GENERAL
William H.H. Miller, 1889

SECRETARY OF THE NAVY
Benjamin F. Tracy, 1889

SECRETARY OF THE INTERIOR
John W. Noble, 1889

SECRETARY OF AGRICULTURE
Jeremiah M. Rusk, 1889

President Benjamin Harrison and his cabinet in 1892. Front row, left to right, Secretary of War Stephen B. Elkins; Secretary of State John W. Foster; President Benjamin Harrison (center); Secretary of the Treasury Charles Foster; and Attorney General William H. H. Miller. Back row, left to right, Secretary of the Interior John W. Noble; Postmaster General John Wanamaker; Secretary of the Navy Benjamin F. Tracy; and Secretary of Agriculture Jeremiah M. Rusk. (Courtesy Library of Congress.)

FAMILY

CHRONOLOGICAL EVENTS

1 October 1832	Caroline Lavinia Scott born	25 October 1892	Caroline Harrison died
20 October 1853	Caroline Lavinia Scott married Benjamin Harrison	6 April 1896	Mary Scott Lord Dimmick married Benjamin Harrison
12 August 1854	Son, Russell, born	21 February 1897	Daughter, Elizabeth, born
3 April 1858	Daughter, Mary (Mamie), born	13 March 1901	Benjamin Harrison died
30 April 1858	Mary Scott Lord born	5 January 1948	Mary Harrison died
1882	Mary Scott Lord married Harrison Dimmick		

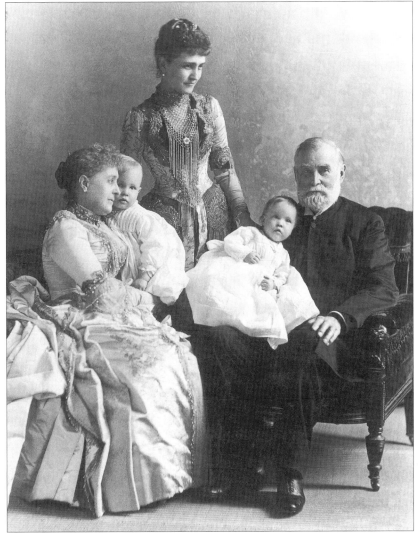

Caroline Lavinia Scott and Benjamin Harrison met when they were teenagers. They were students at her father's school, Farmers' College. The Harrisons had a son and a daughter.

Mary Harrison married J. Robert McKee, a founder of General Electric. This photograph, taken in the White House, shows four generations. The First Lady, Caroline Harrison, is holding her grandson, Benjamin Harrison McKee. The First Lady's father, Dr. John W. Scott, holds his great granddaughter, Mary McKee. The children's mother, Mary McKee, helped her mother as White House hostess. (Courtesy Library of Congress.)

PRESIDENT BENJAMIN HARRISON HOME

1230 North Delaware Street • Indianapolis, Indiana 46202 • Tel: (317) 631-1898

President Harrison conducted one gubernatorial, two senatorial, and two presidential campaigns from his home in Indianapolis, Indiana. He lived there from 1875 until his death in 1901 except for the years he spent in Washington, D.C. (Courtesy President Benjamin Harrison Home.)

Located near the Meridian Street and Pennsylvania Street exits off of I-65. Open Monday through Saturday from 10 A.M. to 3:30 P.M.; Sunday from 12:30 P.M. to 3:30 P.M. Closed Easter, Thanksgiving, Christmas, and the month of January. Admission fee, with discounts available for prearranged group tours. The third floor houses the Harrison Research Library, which is open by appointment, and a display gallery of Harrison's political and personal artifacts. Owned by the Arthur Jordan Foundation, Indianapolis, and preserved as a memorial to President Harrison by the President Benjamin Harrison Foundation.

The President Benjamin Harrison Home was completed in 1875 under the direction of architect H. T. Brandt. Gas lamps and a coal furnace were used for light and heat in this 16-room brick mansion. In the 1890s, Harrison returned from Washington, D.C. and commissioned a major remodeling which included indoor plumbing, electricity, central heating, and a Colonial-style front porch.

After Harrison's death in 1901, his second wife, Mary, moved to New York and rented the family home out as a boarding house. In 1937, Mrs. Harrison sold the home to the Jordan Conservatory of Music, which used it as a dormitory.

In 1966, a nonprofit foundation was established to operate and maintain the Harrison home as a historic site. The foundation worked in conjunction with family members on a full-scale renovation which included the remodeling of the dirt-floor cellar into community meeting rooms.

All the furnishings in the home are original, including the hand-carved wooden bed in which Harrison died. The furniture from his law office, which was located on Market Street in downtown Indianapolis, is also on display there.

The home was opened to the public in 1974.

▲ *The upstairs sitting room connects with the Harrisons' bedroom. The first Mrs. Harrison liked to paint in this room, and one of her paintings is displayed there.* (Courtesy President Benjamin Harrison Home.)

Benjamin Harrison died on 13 March 1901 in the master bedroom of his home in Indianapolis, Indiana. On 16 March, his body lay in state at the Indiana statehouse. Funeral services were conducted the next day. He was buried beside his first wife, Caroline, at Crown Hill Cemetery in Indianapolis. (Courtesy Library of Congress.) ▶

William McKinley

[signature: William M. McKinley]

CHRONOLOGICAL EVENTS

29 January 1843	Born, Niles, Ohio
11 June 1861	Enlisted in the Twenty-third Ohio Volunteer Infantry
17 September 1862	Decorated for his bravery during the Battle of Antietam and promoted to second lieutenant
7 February 1863	Promoted to first lieutenant
25 July 1864	Promoted to captain
14 March 1865	Promoted to brevet major
1866–1867	Attended Albany Law School, New York
5 March 1867	Admitted to bar, Warren, Ohio
5 October 1876	Elected to U.S. House of Representatives; served six terms
1890	Ran unsuccessfully for reelection to U.S. House of Representatives
1891	Elected governor of Ohio
1893	Reelected governor of Ohio
3 November 1896	Elected president
4 March 1897	Inaugurated president
24 July 1897	Signed Dingley Tariff Act
15 February 1898	*U.S.S. Maine* exploded in Havana harbor, Cuba
25 April 1898	War declared against Spain
7 July 1898	Signed joint resolution annexing Hawaiian Islands
10 December 1898	Paris Peace Treaty signed, ending Spanish-American War; ratified 6 February 1899
1899–1900	Authorized Open Door Policy with China
14 March 1900	Signed Gold Standard Act
6 November 1900	Reelected president
4 March 1901	Inaugurated president
6 September 1901	Shot by Leon Czolgosz
14 September 1901	Died, Buffalo, New York

BIOGRAPHY

EARLY CAREER. William McKinley, the twenty-fifth president of the United States, was born in the small town of Niles, Ohio on 29 January 1843. He grew up at a time when the United States was rapidly becoming more industrialized. His future political career would reflect the tensions caused by this shift from a nation of small farmers to a nation of small farmers and factory workers.

McKinley enlisted in the Union army at the start of the Civil War. He served under the command of the future president Rutherford B. Hayes and participated in the brutal battle of Antietam (1862).

McKinley rose to the rank of major by the war's end. After the war, he completed law school and began practicing law in his home state.

His life as a young man was marked by sadness and misfortune. The tragic deaths of his two children left his wife, Ida, an invalid. However, her illness may have helped develop the tremendous patience that would later become one of his greatest political assets.

McKinley's first move into politics came in 1868, when he worked as an aide in the presidential campaign of Ulysses S. Grant. In 1875, his fiery speeches in support of Hayes's campaign for governor of Ohio established McKinley's reputation as an effective speaker. The next year he was elected to the U.S. House of Representatives. Because of his support for a high protective tariff, he immediately became identified with the interests of big business in his home state. In 1880, James A. Garfield was elected president. McKinley succeeded him as a member of the Ways and Means Committee, where he continued his support of the industrial and manufacturing concerns of the country. In 1889, he became chairman of this committee. He soon became recognized as the official Republican leader in the House of Representatives. In 1890, he introduced the McKinley Tariff, the highest peacetime tariff in the history of the United States up to that time.

His career in Congress seemed to come to an end with his defeat in the congressional election of 1890. However, he maintained his visibility as a national politician with his election in 1891 as governor of Ohio and his reelection to that position in 1893. An immensely popular governor, McKinley came to be viewed by his party as a strong candidate for national office, partly because he had no personal enemies, having distanced himself as much as possible from political controversy. Also, he was highly respected by the voters. Consequently, when the Republican Party met in St. Louis in June 1896 to choose its candidate for president, McKinley's nomination on the first ballot surprised no one. His election that year is considered to be one of the most crucial elections ever in the nation's entire history.

THE ELECTION OF 1896. The 1896 election came at a time of national crisis for the United States. The panic of 1893 had developed into the worst depression the nation had suffered. Violence in the 1892 coal miners' strike at Homestead, Pennsylvania, and during the Chicago Pullman strike of 1894 served as strong reminders of the labor unrest that was sweeping through the country.

The unfortunate situation of the poor was highlighted in 1893 when Jacob Coxey of McKinley's home state of Ohio led a well-publicized "poor people's" march on Washington, D.C. Class conflict tore through the cities. Throughout the countryside farmers grew increasingly frustrated at what they perceived to be the unfair business practices of the railroads, which they accused of price gouging (charging too much) as they transported their goods to market. Cities became overrun with crime and millions of new immigrants were forced to live in filthy conditions.

The one question that produced more controversy than any other since the Civil War was the issue of silver. As the effects of the 1893 depression grew harsher, the demand for currency inflation increased. Those people who were deeply in debt favored the expansion of the money supply through the unlimited coinage of silver as a means of producing inflation. They believed that this would raise wages and supposedly ease their debt burden by giving them more money with which to repay their debts. Some economists believed that this would restore the country's prosperity.

The 1896 Republican platform opposed free coinage of silver. Instead, the party supported currency backed by gold. This stand seemed to favor the banking and manufacturing interests of the Northeast, which opposed inflation rather than the farming interests of the South and the West. Furthermore, McKinley named Mark Hanna, an Ohio industrialist, as his campaign manager. Hanna financed the campaign largely through

Jacob Coxey, of Massillon, Ohio, wanted two bills passed that would give work to the unemployed. He left Massillon on Easter Sunday 1894 with about 100 men. He predicted that he would arrive in Washington, D.C. with 100,000 supporters.

Coxey's army only amounted to about 500 men when they arrived at the Capitol for a demonstration on May Day. He was arrested, fined, and sent to jail. Coxey's followers were supported by organized labor and the Populist Party. Other armies of the unemployed arose all over the country. They showed how much economic unrest there was at the time. (Courtesy Library of Congress.)

contributions from big business, thus furthering the belief that McKinley was nothing more than a spokesman for the rich.

The Democratic candidate in 1896 was William Jennings Bryan, the charming and energetic two-term Nebraska congressman who had been defeated in 1894 in his bid for a Senate seat. While McKinley had hoped to run primarily on the issue of the high protective tariffs with which his name had become synonymous, Bryan was able to turn McKinley's defense of the gold standard into the campaign's major issue. Even without this highly charged emotional issue, however, the campaign

would still have been a memorable one. Campaign literature was used extensively and under the capable directorship of Hanna. McKinley's supporters distributed 250 million campaign fliers to voters throughout the country. McKinley ran a brilliantly orchestrated race from his front porch in Canton, Ohio from which he addressed no fewer than three quarters of a million potential voters. His opponent, Bryan, crisscrossing the country on a whirlwind speaking tour, delivered some of the most memorable political speeches in U.S. political history.

"Burn down your cities and leave our farms

[untouched], and your cities will spring up again as if by magic, but destroy our farms and the grass will grow in the streets of every city in the country. . . . You shall not press upon the brow of labor this crown of thorns. You shall not crucify mankind upon a cross of gold," Bryan roared to his supporters throughout the country, igniting the political passions of many of the country's poor rural dwellers. But he could not singlehandedly defeat the army of Republican speakers who traveled the nation in support of McKinley. Also Hanna encouraged a negative image of Bryan, picturing the Democrat as a political radical whose

"communist spirit" posed a threat to the capitalist system of the United States. Predictably, big business also did what it could to ensure McKinley's election. One factory owner informed his employees that, while they were free to vote as they pleased, if Bryan were elected, "the whistle will not blow Wednesday morning."

Even the modest Republican support from the silver mining states of the West was not enough to win the election for Bryan, the young and inexperienced former representative from Nebraska. Voters seemed reassured by McKinley's experience and encouraged by his outstanding reputation for

THE LOCKOUT IS ENDED; HE HOLDS THE KEY.

This McKinley poster from 1896 showed him holding the golden key which would open the temple of prosperity. The two men waving their hats represent labor and capital. (Courtesy Collection of David J. and Janice L. Frent.)

FIRST INAUGURAL ADDRESS

The responsibilities of the high trust to which I have been called—always of grave importance—are augmented by the prevailing business conditions entailing idleness upon willing labor and loss to useful enterprises. The country is suffering from industrial disturbances from which speedy relief must be had. Our financial system needs some revision; our money is all good now, but its value must not further be threatened. It should all be put upon an enduring basis, not subject to easy attack, nor its stability to doubt or dispute. Our currency should continue under the supervision of the government. The several forms of our paper money offer, in my judgment, a constant embarrassment to the government and a safe balance in the treasury. Therefore I believe it necessary to devise a system which, without diminishing the circulating medium or offering a premium for its contraction, will present a remedy for those arrangements which, temporary in their nature, might well in the years of our prosperity have been displaced by wiser provisions. With adequate revenue secured, but not until then, we can enter upon such changes in our fiscal laws as will, while insuring safety and volume to our money, no longer impose upon the government the necessity of maintaining so large a gold reserve, with its attendant and inevitable temptations to speculation. Most of our financial laws are the outgrowth of experience and trial, and should not be amended without investigation and demonstration of the wisdom of the proposed changes. We must be both "sure we are right" and "make haste slowly." If, therefore, Congress, in its wisdom, shall deem it expedient to create a commission to take under early consideration the revision of our coinage, banking and currency laws, and give them that exhaustive, careful and dispassionate examination that their importance demands, I shall cordially concur in such action. If such power is vested in the president, it is my purpose to appoint a commission of prominent, well-informed citizens of different parties, who will command public confidence, both on account of their ability and special fitness for the work. Business experience and public training may thus be combined, and the patriotic zeal of the friends of the country be so directed that such a report will be made as to receive the support of all parties, and our finances cease to be the subject of mere partisan contention. The experiment is, at all events, worth a trial, and, in my opinion, it can but prove beneficial to the entire country.

The question of international bimetallism will have early and earnest attention. It will be my constant endeavor to secure it by cooperation with the other great commercial powers of the world. Until that condition is realized when the parity between our gold and silver money springs from and is supported by the relative value of the two metals, the value of the silver already coined and of that which may hereafter be coined, must be kept constantly at par with gold by every resource at our command. The credit of the government, the integrity of its currency, and the inviolability of its obligations must be preserved. This was the commanding verdict of the people, and it will not be unheeded. . . .

• *The 1896 presidential campaign became the most memorable and exciting since that of 1860. On 4 March 1897, Republican clubs from all over the United States came to Washington to witness McKinley's inauguration. In his address, which he slowly read from folded sheets bearing many last minute corrections, the new President surveyed the country's economic conditions and pledged to improve them through his main campaign promise—"sound money."*

President McKinley ordered the U.S. battleship Maine *from Key West, Florida to Cuba to protect American interests. The* Maine *is shown here arriving in Havana Harbor on the morning of 25 January 1898. It sank on 15 February 1898, killing 266 of the crew of 350. Within an hour of the explosion, the commanding officer, Charles D. Sigsbee, sent a cable to Secretary of the Navy John D. Long: "Public opinion should be suspended until further report." However, cries of "Remember the Maine! To Hell with Spain!" swept the country and President McKinley asked Congress for a declaration of war on 11 April 1898. (Harper's Pictorial* History of the War with Spain, Courtesy Collection of Charles E. Smith.)

MCKINLEY'S WAR MESSAGE

Obedient to that precept of the Constitution which commands the President to give from time to time to the Congress information of the state of the Union and to recommend to their consideration such measures as he shall judge necessary and expedient, it becomes my duty now to address your body with regard to the grave crisis that has arisen in the relations of the United States to Spain by reason of the warfare that for more than three years has raged in the neighboring island of Cuba. . . .

The present revolution is but the successor of other similar insurrections which have occurred in Cuba against the dominion of Spain, extending over a period of nearly half a century, each of which during its progress has subjected the United States to great effort and expense in enforcing its neutrality laws, caused enormous losses to American trade and commerce, caused irritation, annoyance, and disturbance among our citizens, and, by the exercise of cruel, barbarous, and uncivilized practices of warfare, shocked the sensibilities and offended the human sympathies of our people. . . .

The long trial has proved that the object for which Spain has waged the war can not be attained. The fire of insurrection may flame or may smolder with varying seasons, but it has not been and it is plain that it can not be extinguished by present methods. The only hope of relief and repose from a condition which can no longer be endured is the enforced pacification of Cuba. In the name of humanity, in the name of civilization, in behalf of endangered American interests which give us the right and the duty to speak and to act, the war in Cuba must stop.

In view of these facts and of these considerations, I ask the Congress to authorize and empower the President to take measures to secure a full and final termination of hostilities between the Government of Spain and the people of Cuba, and to secure in the island the establishment of a stable government, capable of maintaining order and observing its international obligations, insuring peace and tranquillity and the security of its citizens as well as our own, and to use the military and naval forces of the United States as may be necessary for these purposes. . . .

The issue is now with the Congress. It is a solemn responsibility. I have exhausted every effort to relieve the intolerable condition of affairs which is at our doors. Prepared to execute every obligation imposed upon me by the Constitution and the law, I await your action. . . .

• *President McKinley delivered his war message to Congress on 11 April 1898. Congress responded with a joint resolution of the two houses on 19 April. Congress granted the President the power he requested.*

honesty and good judgment. It also helped him that much of the national press came out in his favor. McKinley's margin of victory, 7.1 million to 6.5 million popular votes and 271 to 176 electoral votes, proved to be the largest winning margin since that of Ulysses S. Grant in 1872. On 4 March 1897, on a clear and mild day in Washington, D.C., dubbed "McKinley weather" by jubilant Republicans, William McKinley was inaugurated as president of the United States.

PRESIDENCY. Although McKinley was elected on the power of a highly emotional domestic issue, it was to be foreign affairs that would dominate his presidency. Throughout most of the late nineteenth century, a majority of Americans displayed little or no concern with foreign affairs. This is not surprising when one considers the intense period of change the country was experiencing,

Congress responded to President McKinley's war message by passing a joint resolution of both houses on 19 April 1898. McKinley sent a telegram to General Stewart L. Woodford, the U.S. minister in Madrid, Spain. The telegram was a demand that Spain would have until 23 April to give a "full and satisfactory response" to the resolution. Before Woodford could deliver the message, Spain said that they considered the resolution to be "equivalent to an evident declaration of war."

McKinley is shown here signing the demand that Spain withdraw its army from Cuba. Representative Joseph Cannon, later Speaker of the House of Representatives, is standing all the way on the left. Secretary of War Russell A. Alger is seated, second from left. (Harper's Pictorial History of the War with Spain, Courtesy Collection of Charles E. Smith.)

changing itself from a rural and agricultural nation to an urban and industrialized one. With the bloodshed of the Civil War still fresh in the nation's memory, its reluctance to get involved in the business of other nations, a policy known as isolationism, becomes even more understandable.

Slowly, however, Americans awoke to the realization that their reluctance to include themselves in world affairs was not suitable for a country apparently on the verge of becoming a great economic and industrial power. The spirit of manifest destiny which had spurred pioneers to carve out a vast continental empire, seemed to be rekindled throughout much of the nation. Many citizens desired expansion far beyond the country's "natural" borders. The purchase of Alaska in 1867 from Russia focused people's attention on the Pacific Ocean, where several European powers, including Great Britain, France, Germany, and Spain, seemed on the threshold of establishing a

Assistant Secretary of the Navy Theodore Roosevelt ordered Commodore George Dewey (left) to the Philippines. He sailed into Manila Bay and, in the early morning hours of 1 May 1898, he gave the order to the captain of his flagship: "You may fire when ready, Gridley." Before noon the Spanish fleet, completely destroyed, surrendered.

General Wesley Merritt (right) was in command of U.S. land forces in the Philippines. On 13 August 1898, he captured the city of Manila. He and Dewey are shown here together on board Dewey's flagship, Olympia.

(*Harper's Pictorial History of the War with Spain,* Courtesy Collection of Charles E. Smith.)

commercial empire well ahead of the United States. These countries had recently undergone an economic change very similar to that occurring in the United States. Many Americans felt that their country could not afford to fall further behind in the search for foreign markets.

Domestic concerns also contributed to this demand for expansion. Although unemployment in the United States was high, a wave of "new" immigration into the United States, primarily from Eastern and Southern Europe, was occurring. With factories already employing as many people as they could, the problem was how to find jobs for these millions of new arrivals. The problem was made greater because industrialization made life on the farm a practical alternative for fewer and fewer people. But how could the factories afford to hire more people, if what they were already producing was exceeding demand? The solution, many people felt, was to open up markets for U.S. products in foreign lands. This would lower unemployment and allow more Americans to live prosperous lives.

Because of the great financial setbacks of the 1890s, this demand for a foreign empire peaked during McKinley's first term in office. Attention focused, however, not on the area of the Pacific Ocean, but rather on Latin America, where the small country of Cuba was under the imperialistic rule of Spain. Several times in the second half of the century, Cubans had tried to rebel against Spanish rule, but each time they were defeated by the more powerful Spanish army. The United States had a growing economic interest in Cuba, primarily because of business investments there in sugar and mining. Gradually the United States came to sympathize with the cause of Cuban independence. When a revolt broke out in February 1895, U.S. sympathy toward the Cubans was so deep that many Americans demanded that the United States actively assist the Cuban rebels. Soon an official Cuban relief headquarters was established in New York to win support for the rebellion.

Public demand for U.S. intervention peaked in February 1898, much of it caused by the pro-war outcries of the popular press, particularly in those papers owned by Joseph Pulitzer and William Randolph Hearst. *The New York Journal*, on 17 February 1898, stated: "We cannot have peace without fighting for it, [so] let us fight and have it over with." To arouse further antagonism toward Spain, the next day it added: "Intervention on behalf of Cuban independence is our duty now. It has even been hastened by events that have reached to the very bottom of the popular heart. . . . The patience of this nation has seemed illimitable. . . . But it has at last been tried too far." Still, the always cautious McKinley hesitated, and Americans grew more and more impatient with his apparent refusal to assist the oppressed people of Cuba. Even his assistant secretary of the navy, Theodore Roosevelt, who would later be McKinley's vice president and succeed him in office, commented that the President was "white-

---

TREATY OF PEACE WITH SPAIN

Article I. Spain relinquishes all claim of sovereignty over and title to Cuba. . . .

Article II. Spain cedes to the United States the island of Porto Rico (sic) and other islands now under Spanish sovereignty in the West Indies, and the island of Guam in the Marianas or Ladrones.

Article III. Spain cedes to the United States the archipelago known as the Philippine Islands. . . .

The United States will pay to Spain the sum of twenty million dollars ($20,000,000) within three months after the exchange of the ratifications of the present treaty. . . .

• *The peace treaty with Spain was concluded in Paris, France on 10 December 1898.*

This 1900 campaign poster shows McKinley and vice presidential candidate Theodore Roosevelt. It compares what the country was like in 1896 under the Democrats with what it had become in 1900 under McKinley and the Republicans. (Courtesy Collection of David J. and Janice L. Frent.)

livered," possessing "no more backbone than a chocolate eclair."

The event which reached "to the bottom of the popular heart" was an explosion aboard the U.S. battleship *Maine* in Havana harbor on the evening of 15 February which caused the deaths of 266 U.S. sailors. While it was never definitively proven that the Spanish were behind the explosion, almost immediately cries of "Remember the Maine! To Hell with Spain!" echoed throughout the country. With the U.S. public now calling for revenge, the still reluctant McKinley asked Congress for a declaration of war against Spain on 11 April 1898. Spain had announced a unilateral cease fire in Cuba, as well as a declaration of its intentions to allow Cuba to establish an independent govern-

ment. While it was McKinley's decision as chief executive to lead the United States into its first war outside its continental limits, it is easy to conclude that he was reacting to the overwhelming sentiment in the country in favor of war, much of it created by an overzealous national press.

The actual war against Spain was mercifully a short one, more because of the lack of skill of the Spanish forces than because of the professionalism of the U.S. Army of 17,000 troops. Among them was a group of Rough Riders best remembered for the bold leadership of then Lieutenant Colonel Theodore Roosevelt. McKinley, once he got past his hesitancy about entering the war, devoted so much of his time to its day-to-day operations that the secretary of war, Russell A.

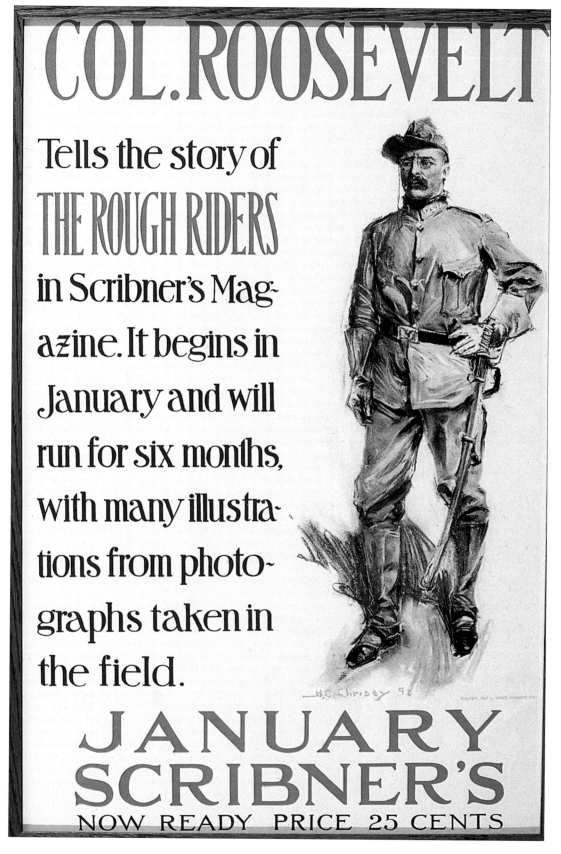

Scribner's magazine issued this advertising poster. The nomination of Theodore Roosevelt to replace the deceased vice president, Garret Hobart, strengthened the Republican ticket in 1900. (Courtesy David J. and Janice L. Frent.)

President McKinley went on a good-will tour after the election of 1900. He was greeted by enthusiastic crowds everywhere. He is shown here speaking in front of a midwestern court house. (Courtesy National Archives.)

Alger, resigned bitterly. Alger claimed that his services were not required with such a "hands-on" president. Hostilities lasted less than four months, and included only two major land battles and one minor sea skirmish. The war stretched into the Pacific Ocean, where a squadron of U.S. battleships under the command of Commodore George Dewey destroyed a Spanish fleet in Manila Bay in the Philippines. Although U.S. casualties were listed as 5,462, only 379 of these were due to injuries sustained in battle; the rest were caused by disease: malaria, dysentery, and yellow fever. The armistice ending the war was signed on 12 August 1898.

But peace proved more difficult than war to President McKinley. After the peace treaty was signed by the two warring nations in December 1898, the United States found itself in the awkward position of having accepted possession of a foreign country, the Philippines, located more than 2,000 miles off its western shore. The question of what to do with the islands quickly dominated the national agenda, almost to the same extent that the issue of war with Spain had six months earlier. The business community wanted to annex the islands, seeing them as a potential stepping-stone to the lucrative Chinese market. Missionary societies urged the same action, claiming to be driven by a wish to save Philippine souls. But how the United States could justify the annexation of one country as a result of a war fought to bring about the liberation of another country (Cuba) was a problem that troubled McKinley.

The reluctance of the United States to either annex or free the Philippines angered the people of the island nation, who now viewed themselves as victims of not Spanish imperialism but U.S. imperialism. Predictably, war soon broke out on the islands, but this was a war that far outlasted the United States's entanglement with Spain. Fighting was brutal, the war was a long one, and casualties were heavy. Finally, with the passage of the Philippine Government Act in July 1902, the nation was declared an "unorganized territory" of the United States, although its inhabitants were declared citizens of the Philippines. It did not achieve full independence until 4 July 1946.

Americans' thirst for empire continued unchecked during the remainder of McKinley's presidency. The Hawaiian Islands were annexed in 1898, putting an end to the hostilities that had existed between the two countries as a result of economic hardships on the islands. These were largely caused by the McKinley Tariff of 1890, which ended many trade concessions previously enjoyed by the islanders. This annexation came under attack by McKinley's critics. They claimed that this new political arrangement would benefit only the large sugar planters on the island, who would profit from new trade guidelines and that it violated the desire for true independence shared by most Hawaiians. Also in the Pacific, with the end of tripartite rule in the Samoan Islands by Germany, Great Britain, and France, the United States in 1899 added part of this island chain, including the harbor of Pago Pago, to its growing empire. With the dawn of a new century, the new-found influence of the United States could be felt as far away as China.

In 1900, Secretary of State John Hay announced to the world that China was open to trade with all countries on an equal basis (the so-called Open Door Policy), thereby upsetting the imperialist designs of the United States's European competitors. Soon, however, Chinese resentment resulted in the Boxer Rebellion, and McKinley was forced to send 2,500 U.S. troops to China as part of the international relief expedition to rescue Western diplomats caught in the surge of Chinese nationalism.

All this activity represented an astounding change in policy for a country that four years earlier had little or nothing to do with the politics of foreign nations. That this change in attitude was in large part engineered by a man as cautious and careful as McKinley makes it even more remarkable. Consequently, when the presidential election of 1900 pitted the same two men against each other, Bryan tried to win the election on the

MCKINLEY'S RECIPROCITY SPEECH

Trade statistics indicate that this country is in a state of unexampled prosperity. The figures are almost appalling. They show that we are utilizing our fields and forests and mines, and that we are furnishing profitable employment to the millions of working-men throughout the United States, bringing comfort and happiness to their homes, and making it possible to lay by savings for old age and disability. That all the people are participating in this great prosperity is seen in every American community, and shown by the enormous and unprecedented deposits in our savings banks. . . .

We have a vast and intricate business, built up through years of toil and struggle, in which every part of the country has its stake, which will not permit either of neglect or of undue selfishness. No narrow, sordid, policy will subserve it. The greatest skill and wisdom on the part of manufacturers and producers will be required to hold and increase it. Our industrial enterprises, which have grown to such proportions, affect the homes and occupations of the people and the welfare of the country. Our capacity to produce has developed so enormously, and our products have so multiplied, that the problem of more markets requires our urgent and immediate attention. Only a broad and enlightened policy will keep what we have. No other policy will get more. In these times of marvelous business energy and gain we ought to be looking to the future, strengthening the weak places in our industrial and commercial systems, that we may be ready for any storm or strain.

By sensible trade arrangements which will not interrupt our home production, we shall extend the outlets for our increasing surplus. A system which provides a mutual exchange of commodities is manifestly essential to the continued and healthful growth of our export trade. We must not repose in fancied security that we can forever sell everything and buy little or nothing. If such a thing were possible, it would not be the best for us or for those with whom we deal. We should take from our customers such of their products as we can use without harm to our industries and labor. Reciprocity is the natural outgrowth of our wonderful industrial development under the domestic policy now firmly established. What we produce beyond our domestic consumption must have a vent abroad. The excess must be relieved through a foreign outlet, and we should sell everywhere we can and buy wherever the buying will enlarge our sales and production, and thereby make a greater demand for home labor.

The period of exclusiveness is past. The expansion of our trade and commerce is the pressing problem. Commercial wars are unprofitable. A policy of good will and friendly trade relations will prevent reprisals. Reciprocity treaties are in harmony with the spirit of the times; measures of retaliation are not. . . .

• *By 1900, the United States passed Great Britain to become the world's leading industrial nation. Republicans credited protective tariffs for this achievement—that is, a tax on imported goods to protect the U.S. manufacturer in the exploding U.S. marketplace without foreign competition. In McKinley's last public speech, he suggested a major modification of this policy—reciprocity, a mutual lowering of tariffs by nations.*

issue of imperialism, portraying the United States's hostilities with Spain as an "unnecessary war." He claimed that the nation's activities abroad were of doubtful moral value and insisted that a great democratic nation such as the United States should not deprive other countries of the

McKinley was the last president to be a Civil War veteran. During his administration, Cuba and the Philippines were freed from Spanish oppression and the Hawaiian Islands were annexed. Fifty one years later, Hawaii became the 50th state admitted to the Union. (Courtesy National Archives.)

same right of self-government. Bryan argued that the money spent on these overseas ventures could have been better spent at home, a theme that would continue to be heard throughout the twentieth century.

Bryan's message fell on deaf ears. The four years of McKinley's administration had generally been prosperous ones for the United States, and McKinley's claim that this prosperity was the result of the protectionist policies of his administration was well received by U.S. workers. Meanwhile, the joy after the military victories of 1898 was still sweeping the country. The Republicans, by nominating Theodore Roosevelt, the fiery governor of New York and the hero of the Rough Riders, to replace deceased Vice President Garret Hobart on the ticket, continued to remind the country of the thrill of foreign conquest. In many ways Bryan proved to be his own worst enemy. Realizing that he had missed out on the issue of imperialism, he tried once again to unify the voters on the silver question and then on the tariff issue. Bryan presented to the American public the image of a desperate politician who stood for nothing rather than that of a respectable man committed to the ideal of a decent nation made up of decent people. The result was a McKinley victory by an even greater margin than his last one. The President received 7.2 to 6.4 million popular votes and received 292 to 155 votes in the Electoral College. In the process, he became the first U.S. president in 28 years to win a second consecutive term.

When McKinley set out on a good-will tour to win support for his new presidency, he was feeling quite confident about the future of the United States. With foreign relations free from complications and prosperity at home rising, he had good reasons for his confidence. The tour carried him first to the Pacific Coast and then, in an attempt to end the sectionalism left over from the Civil War, to the Southern states. Wherever he went, he was greeted by enthusiastic crowds. His triumphant tour continued in Buffalo, New York, which he visited in September 1901 to deliver a set of speeches at the Pan-American Exposition that was assembling there. His message was well received and seemed to indicate that the United States was comfortable in its new role of world leadership. "Isolation is no longer possible or desirable. The period of exclusiveness is past," roared the President to an eager crowd.

Tragedy, however, awaited him. On 6 September, as McKinley was attending a reception at the exposition, Leon Czolgosz, an anarchist who later claimed to believe in the assassination of world leaders, shot him at point-blank range with a revolver. Although McKinley appeared to be recuperating, he collapsed and died eight days later, becoming the fifth U.S. president to die in office and the third to be assassinated. The assassin was later convicted of his crime and executed. The slain President was survived by his wife, Ida, of 34 years, and, amid a huge display of public sympathy, was buried in Canton, Ohio on 19 September 1901.

SUMMARY. William McKinley led his country through a period of strong change, and his election in 1896 represented the victory of urban over rural America. Likewise, under the guidance of Mark Hanna, McKinley's presidency ushered in the permanent influence of corporate America into the U.S. political system.

McKinley's critics claim that because he was personally indebted to his friend and benefactor Mark Hanna, he was nothing more than a spokesman for big business. His continued defense of high tariffs, according to these critics, serves as ample evidence of his constant preference to favor the rich over the poor. Likewise, the accusation that the U.S. annexation of overseas territory, dubbed imperialism, burdened the country with needless responsibilities and alliances that were contrary to the ideals of universal democracy.

To McKinley's defenders, however, he announced to the world that the United States was willing, eager, and able to accept the responsibilities that came with being one of the world's great economic powers. Not only did he free Cuba and the Philippines from Spanish oppression; he also paved the way for the establishment of democracy in the Hawaiian Islands. This process would result in the island nation's admittance into the Union in 1959 as the 50th state.

McKinley governed during a period of domestic prosperity. As president, he displayed an unusual flexibility of thought, evidenced by his talent for picking good and capable people to advise him, while never losing sight of the fact that it was he and not they who was the nation's chosen leader. He was a man who clearly accepted responsibility for his actions. Although not a man of great personal magnetism, he was man of much dignity who was liked and respected by friends and foes alike. A friendly, congenial, and sympathetic man who inspired loyalty and trust from his colleagues, McKinley, beyond being a leader of the American people, was their chosen representative.

His greatest triumph, however, is the strong modern presidency, in which the country's chief executive would lead rather than follow. This tradition began with his term of office and would expand even further with such dynamic leaders as Theodore Roosevelt and Franklin D. Roosevelt, presidents who left permanent marks on their country. In judging McKinley, then, it is wise to consider the reaction to his untimely death, which was genuine and prolonged national mourning. It stands as perhaps the best, and the most accurate, measurement of the man to whom it was a tribute.

VICE PRESIDENT

Garret Augustus Hobart
(1844–1899)

CHRONOLOGICAL EVENTS

1844	Born, Long Branch, New Jersey, 3 June
1863	Graduated from Rutgers College, New Jersey
1871	Appointed city counsel of Paterson, New Jersey
1872	Elected to New Jersey Assembly
1896	Elected vice president
1899	Died, Paterson, New Jersey, 21 November

BIOGRAPHY

A schoolteacher's son, Garret Augustus "Gus" Hobart attended his father's school in Long Branch, New Jersey. He graduated first in his class from Rutgers College and studied law with a Republican lawyer, Socrates Tuttle, in Paterson, New Jersey. Hobart later married Tuttle's daughter, Jennie, and also switched to his political party.

Tuttle became mayor of Paterson and appointed his son-in-law city counsel. Hobart went on to the state assembly, where he became speaker, and to the state senate, where he served as senate president. At the same time, he carried on a thriving law practice, serving many banking and railroad clients who made him wealthy. He failed, however, in several attempts to win election to the U.S. Senate.

From 1880 to 1891, Hobart served as chairman of the New Jersey Republican Committee and was a member of the national Republican Committee. Compensating for his lack of national office, these positions earned him recognition within his party. In 1896, the Republican Party nominated Ohio Governor William McKinley for president and chose Hobart for vice president, since New Jersey was a critical "swing state." Hobart anguished over the nomination, knowing all that it meant "in work, worry, and loss of home and bliss."

In Washington, Vice President Hobart and his family moved into the "Little Cream White House" across from the White House. Because Mrs. McKinley was an invalid, the Hobarts took over much of the President's social entertaining. President McKinley frequently attended Hobart's dinners. The two men became such close and trusted friends that Hobart was called the "assistant president." He even handled some of McKinley's personal finances.

Vice President Hobart presided over the debates leading to the Spanish-American War in 1898. He cast the tie-breaking vote to claim the Philippines as a U.S. colony. When Secretary of War Russell A. Alger became an embarrassment to the administration because of cheap and inferior goods supplied to U.S. troops during the war, the genial McKinley could not fire his friend. Instead, Vice President Hobart took Alger aside and convinced him to submit his resignation.

Early in 1899, Hobart developed a serious heart ailment that drained him of energy. Deeply alarmed, President McKinley invited the Hobarts to stay at the White House. Instead, Hobart returned to New Jersey, he died in November, leaving the vice presidency vacant until it was filled in McKinley's second term by Theodore Roosevelt.

VICE PRESIDENT

Theodore Roosevelt
(1858–1919)

CHRONOLOGICAL EVENTS

1858	Born, New York, New York, 27 October
1880	Graduated from Harvard College, Cambridge, Massachusetts
1881	Elected to New York State Assembly
1897	Appointed assistant secretary of the navy
1898	Organized Rough Riders to fight in Cuba
1898	Elected governor of New York
1900	Elected vice president
1901	Became president upon the death of William McKinley
1904	Elected president
1919	Died, Oyster Bay, New York, 6 January

BIOGRAPHY

Suffering from severe childhood asthma, Theodore Roosevelt exercised to improve his physical fitness. By the time he entered Harvard College, he had become an athlete and an enthusiastic outdoorsman.

At age 23, he won election to the New York State Assembly. A reform-minded Republican, Roosevelt helped pass civil service and other reform legislation supported by Democratic Governor Grover Cleveland. Distraught over the deaths of his wife and mother, Roosevelt gave up political office to hunt and run a cattle ranch in the Dakota Territory.

Roosevelt returned in 1886 to run a losing race for mayor of New York. He then served as civil service commissioner and as New York police commissioner. In 1897, he became assistant secretary of the navy. When the United States declared war on Spain, he resigned to raise a volunteer regiment popularly known as the Rough Riders. Their well-publicized exploits in Cuba helped him to be elected governor of New York after the war.

As governor, Roosevelt often sided with reformers against the machine politicians. The state's Republican boss, Thomas C. Platt, sought to rid himself of Roosevelt by having him nominated for vice president in 1900. Although Roosevelt insisted that he did not want the job, the convention teamed him with the incumbent president, William McKinley.

McKinley stayed home and conducted a "front porch" campaign while Roosevelt toured the country giving speeches. The Republicans won easily. A man of action, Roosevelt seemed unsuited for the confinement of the vice presidency. But he occupied the office for only six months before President McKinley was assassinated. Roosevelt went on to become an active and popular president. His support for conservation, consumer legislation, and enforcement of the antitrust laws energized the Progressive movement, and his foreign policy thrust the United States into world affairs. Winning election as president in 1904, he retired in 1908 after his second term. Drawn steadily into the reform camp, Roosevelt broke with his successor, William Howard Taft, and ran as the Progressive (Bull Moose) Party candidate for president in 1912. Roosevelt and Taft both lost to the Democratic nominee, Woodrow Wilson.

THE CABINET

SECRETARY OF STATE
John Sherman, 1897
William R. Day, 1898
John M. Hay, 1898, 1901

SECRETARY OF WAR
Russell A. Alger, 1897
Elihu Root, 1899, 1901

SECRETARY OF THE TREASURY
Lyman J. Gage, 1897, 1901

POSTMASTER GENERAL
James A. Gary, 1897
Charles Emory Smith, 1898, 1901

ATTORNEY GENERAL
Joseph McKenna, 1897
John W. Griggs, 1898, 1901
Philander C. Knox, 1901

SECRETARY OF THE NAVY
John D. Long, 1897

SECRETARY OF THE INTERIOR
Cornelius N. Bliss, 1897
Ethan A. Hitchcock, 1899, 1901

SECRETARY OF AGRICULTURE
James Wilson, 1897

(Courtesy Rutherford B. Hayes Presidential Center, Fremont, Ohio.)

John Sherman (1823–1900). Sherman was appointed secretary of state by President William McKinley in 1897. He had previously served as secretary of the treasury during the administration of Rutherford B. Hayes. He also served in the U.S. House of Representatives (1855–1861) and in the U.S. Senate (1862–1877).

As a senator from Ohio, Sherman sponsored the Sherman Antitrust Act (1890), which prohibited industrial monopolies in "restraint of trade or commerce." The same year he supported the Sherman Silver Purchase Act (1890), which required the U.S. Treasury to purchase 4.5 million ounces of silver at the market price. The silver was purchased with Treasury notes that could be redeemed in gold. This law was repealed in 1893 because it drained the federal gold reserves.

Sherman was very ill and was unable to carry out most of his duties as secretary of state. He disagreed with President McKinley on going to war with Spain and resigned in 1898. Sherman was replaced by his assistant secretary, William R. Day.

President McKinley and the War Cabinet, 1898. President McKinley (far left); clockwise from McKinley's left, Secretary of the Treasury Lyman J. Gage; Attorney General John W. Griggs; Secretary of the Navy John D. Long; (standing) Secretary of Agriculture James Wilson and Secretary of the Interior Cornelius N. Bliss; Postmaster General Charles Emory Smith; Secretary of War Russell A. Alger and Secretary of State William R. Day (seated on McKinley's right).

This photograph was taken in the Cabinet Room of the Executive Mansion in 1898. (Harper's Pictorial History of the War with Spain, Volume I , Courtesy Collection Charles E. Smith.)

FAMILY

CHRONOLOGICAL EVENTS

8 June 1847	Ida Saxton born	14 September 1901	William McKinley died
25 January 1871	Ida Saxton married William McKinley	26 May 1907	Ida McKinley died

(Courtesy Library of Congress.)

Ida Saxton's father was a prominent banker in Canton, Ohio. She was well-educated, and she worked in her father's bank for awhile. She met William McKinley at a picnic in 1867. They were married two years later, after she returned from a European tour.

Two daughters died in childhood. Ida McKinley was seriously ill with epilepsy for 20 years before she moved into the White House. She was totally dependent on the President who took excellent care of her. After his assassination, she visited his grave almost every day. Her younger sister took care of her until her death.

THE McKINLEY MEMORIAL AND MUSEUM

800 McKinley Monument Drive, NW • Canton, Ohio 44708-4800 • Tel: (216) 455-7043

In the summer of 1901, the McKinleys visited their Canton home before traveling to the Pan-American Exposition in Buffalo, New York, where the President was shot by Leon Czolgosz. After the services in Buffalo and in Washington, D.C., the president's body was returned for the last time to the home before the 19 September funeral in Canton, Ohio. The home has since been demolished. (Courtesy The McKinley Museum.)

Located off I-77 South at Exit 106, or I-77 North at Exit 105, approximately 20 miles southeast of Akron. Open Monday through Saturday from 9 A.M. to 5 P.M., and Sunday from 12 P.M. to 5 P.M. Summer hours: Monday through Saturday from 9 A.M. to 7 P.M., and Sunday from 12 P.M. to 7 P.M. The site contains the McKinley National Memorial Monument; a Museum of History, Science and Industry; the Ramsayer Research Library; and the Hoover–Price Planetarium. Admission fee for the museum; the planetarium is free with admission to the museum. Group reservations should be made three weeks in advance by contacting the museum at (216) 455-7043. Private showings may be arranged for groups of 20 or more. Owned and maintained by the Stark County Historical Society.

President William McKinley was shot by an anarchist while attending a reception at the Pan-American Exposition in Buffalo, New York on 6 September 1901. He died eight days later. His body was interred at the Werts Memorial Vault in Canton's Westlawn Cemetery until 1907, when it was moved to the McKinley National Memorial Monument. His wife, Ida, and two children, Katherine and Ida, were also laid to rest there.

The McKinley National Memorial Association

was formed on 26 September 1901, and a site was soon chosen for the monument. To help in raising funds, Ohio Governor George K. Nash proclaimed McKinley's birthday (29 January) a day of observance by that state's schools. By June 1903, contributions reached $500,000, and the association was able to purchase 26 acres from the Cemetery Association and adjacent property owners. Over 60 designs were submitted for the proposed monument. The Association chose a plan submitted by Harold Van Buren Magonigle of New York. He proposed a mausoleum designed in the shape of a cross and sword (when seen from above). The cross symbolizes McKinley's martyrdom, and the sword his service as Commander in Chief during wartime.

After the dedication ceremony on 30 September 1907, the McKinley National Memorial Association continued to maintain the monument and grounds until 1943. At that time the property was transferred to the Ohio State Archaeological and Historical Society. Thirty years later, the memorial was transferred to the Stark County Historical Society, which funded a restoration project for the monument and grounds. The McKinley National Memorial Monument was rededicated on 26 September 1992. The grounds feature the McKinley Museum, which houses the largest known collection of McKinley memorabilia and exhibits that help document American history.

It is estimated that more than one million school children from around the world donated money to construct the McKinley Memorial Monument. (Courtesy The McKinley Museum.)

SUGGESTED READING

RUTHERFORD B. HAYES

Neal E. Robbins's *Rutherford B. Hayes* (Garrett Educational Corp., 1989) is a well-done introductory biography. (For junior and senior high school.)

Keith I. Polakoff's *The Politics of Inertia* (Louisiana State University Press, 1973), while not really a biography, analyzes the election of 1876, the Compromise of 1877, which resulted in Hayes's presidency, and the development of the two-party system. *The Presidency of Rutherford B. Hayes* by Ari Hoogenboom (University Press of Kansas, 1988) is an excellent political biography of Hayes. Emily A. Geer's *First Lady, The Life of Lucy Webb Hayes* (Kent State University Press, 1984) is a delightful biography. Lucy Hayes was the first president's wife to be referred to as the First Lady, and she was the first to use that position to advance charitable causes. She was known as Lemonade Lucy because of the temperance policy that prevailed in the White House during her years as First Lady. (For high school and adult.)

JAMES A. GARFIELD

Fern G. Brown's *James A. Garfield* (Garrett Educational Corp., 1990) is a good general biography. Edwin P. Hoyt's *James A. Garfield* (Reilly & Lee, 1964) emphasizes his congressional leadership and discusses the problems of the Reconstruction era. (For junior and senior high school.)

Hendrik Booraem's *The Road to Respectability: James A. Garfield and His World, 1844–1852* (Western Reserve Historical Society, 1988) is well written but deals only with his adolescence and his growing up into a young man in rural Ohio. *Garfield of Ohio* by John M. Taylor (Norton, 1970) describes his developing leadership skills as a general during the Civil War. *James A. Garfield: His Life and Times* by Richard L. McElroy (Daring Book, 1986) is an excellent compilation of photographs. The narrative fits the photos well. Allan Peskin's *Garfield* (Kent State University Press, 1978) is a well-done, full-scale biography that emphasizes his political career before his ill-fated four-month presidency. (For high school and adult.)

CHESTER A. ARTHUR

Rita Stevens's *Chester A. Arthur* (Garrett Educational Corp., 1989) is a well-done introductory study. (For junior and senior high school.)

Thomas C. Reeves's *Gentleman Boss: The Life of Chester Alan Arthur* (Knopf, 1975) is an excellent full-scale biography. *The Presidencies of James A. Garfield and Chester A. Arthur* by Justus Doenecke (Regents Press of Kansas, 1981) provides insight into the development of both domestic and foreign policy during what was called the Gilded Age. (For high school and adult.)

GROVER CLEVELAND

Edwin P. Hoyt's *Grover Cleveland* (Reilly & Lee, 1962) is a good general biography of the only president to serve two nonconsecutive terms in office. (For junior high school.)

Grover Cleveland by David R. Collins (Garrett Educational Corp., 1988) is an excellent introductory biography. (For junior and senior high school.)

Rexford G. Tugwell's *Grover Cleveland* (Macmillan, 1968) is a fairly well-balanced biography. It includes a detailed chronology of his career. Allan Nevins's *Grover Cleveland* (Dodd, Mead, 1941) is a Pulitzer Prize–winning volume on Cleveland and the Gilded Age. (For high school and adult.)

BENJAMIN HARRISON

Elisabeth P. Myers's *Benjamin Harrison* (Reilly & Lee, 1969) is a well-done introductory biography of the grandson of William Henry Harrison. (For junior high school.)

Benjamin Harrison by Rita Stevens (Garrett Educational Corp., 1989) is a good general biography. (For junior and senior high school.)

The Presidency of Benjamin Harrison by Homer E. Socolofsky (University Press of Kansas, 1987) is a well-researched work that analyzes Harrison's contributions such as a more assertive foreign policy and a more efficient executive branch. (For high school and adult.)

WILLIAM McKINLEY

Edwin P. Hoyt's *William McKinley* (Reilly & Lee, 1967) is a well-done introductory biography. David R. Collins's *William McKinley* (Garrett Educational Corp., 1990) presents a well-balanced picture of the president. (For junior and senior high school.)

William McKinley and His America by H. Wayne Morgan (Syracuse University Press, 1963) emphasizes the political life of McKinley and his foreign relations policies. Included is a discussion of the Spanish-American War, which resulted in the acquisition by the United States of the Philippines and other islands in the Pacific. *The Presidency of William McKinley* by Lewis L. Gould (University Press of Kansas, 1981) is an excellent political biography. (For high school and adult.)

at a glance . . .

President	Volume	President	Volume	President	Volume
George Washington	1	James Buchanan	3	Calvin Coolidge	5
John Adams	1	Abraham Lincoln	3	Herbert Hoover	5
Thomas Jefferson	1	Andrew Johnson	3	Franklin D. Roosevelt	6
James Madison	1	Ulysses S. Grant	3	Harry S. Truman	6
James Monroe	1	Rutherford B. Hayes	4	Dwight D. Eisenhower	6
John Quincy Adams	2	James A. Garfield	4	John F. Kennedy	6
Andrew Jackson	2	Chester A. Arthur	4	Lyndon B. Johnson	6
Martin Van Buren	2	Grover Cleveland	4	Richard M. Nixon	7
William Henry Harrison	2	Benjamin Harrison	4	Gerald R. Ford	7
John Tyler	2	William McKinley	4	Jimmy Carter	7
James K. Polk	2	Theodore Roosevelt	5	Ronald Reagan	7
Zachary Taylor	3	William Howard Taft	5	George Bush	7
Millard Fillmore	3	Woodrow Wilson	5	Bill Clinton	7
Franklin Pierce	3	Warren G. Harding	5		

Tammany Hall, 46, 75–76
Tilden, Samuel J. 3, 5

Vice presidents,
   Arthur, Chester A., 23, 31–33
   Hendricks, Thomas Andrews, 63
   Hobart, Garret Augustus, 107
   Morton, Levi Parsons, 83
   Roosevelt, Theodore, 98, 103, 108
   Stevenson, Adlai Ewing, 64
   Wheeler, William Almon, 13

Wheeler, William Almon, 13